SAINT AND

Merry Christmas 2008.

Mr. Brian Sellars
32 Leysholme Crescent
Leeds
West Yorkshire
LS12 4HJ   185619 / 33400
World Cancer Research Fund
www.wcrf-uk.org/learn

SAINT AND SINNER

THE AUTOBIOGRAPHY
OF A RUGBY LEAGUE LEGEND

ALEX MURPHY OBE

MAINSTREAM
PUBLISHING

EDINBURGH AND LONDON

First published in Great Britain in 2000 by
MAINSTREAM PUBLISHING COMPANY (EDINBURGH) LTD
7 Albany Street
Edinburgh EH1 3UG

This edition 2002

ISBN 1 84018 309 8

A catalogue record for this book is available from the British Library

Typeset in Impact and Janson Text
Printed and bound by Antony Rowe, Eastbourne

Contents

ONE

A bad day at the office

The crumpled figure lying in an undignified heap on the office floor didn't look much like a winner. A peach of a right hook had sent him sprawling, dumped him flat on his backside.

That punch not only ended a ten-year friendship, it brought down the curtain on the job of a lifetime and was the spark that launched one of sport's greatest empire-builders on his road to fame. Versions of what happened on that July day in 1984 have varied between tales of attempted bare-handed strangulation to suggestions that I tried to choke the Wigan chairman with his own telephone cord.

It is impossible to spend more than forty years in a job or a sport without having a run-in or two with the bosses, and I have had more than my share since I first signed professional forms for St Helens on my sixteenth birthday.

But the most far-reaching and dramatic of them all was the row with Maurice Lindsay in the privacy of his own office –

a bust-up that stunned the world of rugby league and turned long-standing friends into bitter enemies.

And it is not too fanciful to suggest that it was instrumental in turning small-town bookie Lindsay into one of the most powerful men in British sport. I firmly believe that it gave him the opportunity he was looking for – to ditch me, to put new men in charge of the team and then to hog the headlines as Wigan continued the climb that I had started. I didn't know it then, but I later came to believe I was a pawn in his scheme all along. I had served my purpose and it was time for Maurice to move on without me. From then it was only a matter of time before he left Wigan to become the chief executive of rugby league and the managing director of Super League, chairman of the ill-fated International Board of Super League with a voice on the Sports Council's Sponsorship and Spectator body and was within a whisker of becoming the head of horseracing's Tote. And it became a burden that I had to bear; I'd like to make the following apology to everybody involved in the sport of rugby league – I was the one who introduced him to the game!

Maurice tells wonderful stories about how, as a starry-eyed youngster, he used stand alone on the terraces of Central Park and watch the great Billy Boston in action. It was the sort of story that went down well with hard-headed rugby league folk who are always unreasonably suspicious of latter-day converts. I still have my doubts, though. The truth, I suspect, is a little different. I wonder if Maurice ever set eyes on Billy Boston until long after the great man had retired and was pulling pints in his pub only a few yards from the old Wigan ground.

Maurice was a small-time rails bookmaker at Bolton dog

track and he spent a lot of time in the group of which I was a part. There were up to ten of us at a time who used to gather together at the track, go for a meal and chat about dogs, horses and the like. Rugby league was not on the agenda and Maurice never once offered an opinion about the game.

Gradually, though, he and I got to know each other better. I used to leave tickets for him on the door at Warrington and eventually I even arranged for him to accompany the team to Wembley for the Challenge Cup final. I am sure that was his first taste of the inside of big-time rugby league.

It was during that period that I had a lot of success – and Maurice loved being part of it. He enjoyed the reflected glory and it was no problem for me because after winning the League Leaders Trophy with Warrington in 1973 I took the side to unprecedented success by winning the Challenge Cup at Wembley, the John Player Trophy, the Captain Morgan Trophy (a one-off competition for the season's élite clubs) and the Club Merit Award. A year later I took Warrington back to Wembley and, although we lost to Widnes in the 1975 final, I was still enjoying success as a coach. In the same year I coached England to runners-up spot in the World Championship and in 1978 Warrington again won the John Player Trophy.

Maurice and I were still close friends when I moved to Salford which, to be honest, was not the great success I had hoped it would be. Salford were the glamour boys of the game, a team stuffed with ex-rugby union stars, but they had under-achieved since winning the First Division Cham-pionship in successive years in the mid-1970s.

It didn't work out and I went back to Leigh where I guided them to their first-ever Championship – to go with their first-ever Challenge Cup win that I had coached them to eleven years earlier. I assume it was that success more than any other that prompted Maurice to offer me the coaching job at Wigan. He had moved in as the head – in style if not in name – of a four-man board whose job was to bring back the great days to Central Park.

I was warned off the move by one member of that small group of friends who told me in front of Maurice: 'Don't take the job.' When Maurice asked him why, he said simply, 'Because I wouldn't trust you even though you say you are a friend.'

But Wigan was far too big a challenge to turn down and when you are offered the position by a man you consider a friend, you don't say no. So, in June 1982, I left Leigh for the second time and moved in at Central Park.

Everything went well at first. Wigan hadn't won a thing for nine years – and the last pot was only the Lancashire Cup. They had even been dumped into the Second Division . . . something that was almost unthinkable. They were still living on memories. Their last championship win had been in 1971 and their latest Challenge Cup victory even further back – 1965.

So to win the John Player Trophy in my first year and to reach Wembley – where we lost to Widnes – didn't seem too bad a start. But it was clear that Maurice Lindsay had bigger plans and they did not include me. I suppose I should have seen it coming. I believed that if Wigan were ever to become a force in the game again there had to be changes. I needed help. A coach can only do so much. He cannot be running off the training pitch to answer phone calls, talk to the press and look after every player's individual needs and fitness without assistance.

I approached Maurice with the idea of beefing up the backroom staff. His response was hardly encouraging. If I was given such help, he suggested, what exactly would I be doing? Not quite what I had hoped to hear but clearly food for thought for my chairman (I was no sooner out of the door than he saw the need to take on fitness coaches, sprint coaches, forward coaches – in fact a whole army of helpers – and claimed the innovative idea as his own).

Things eventually came to a head on the day of the Wigan Sevens. But, let's get the record straight – I did *not* try to strangle him with his own telephone cord. It's true, he ended up in a bundle on the office floor and the telephone was in his lap. But what put him there was a straight old-fashioned punch. All these years later I still believe he deserved it. And it was all over a paltry twenty pounds that was going to charity anyway . . .

We had won the Sevens event but more than an hour after the final I had still not clapped eyes on Maurice, which was most unusual because he liked to be seen around winners and, even though it was only a Charity Sevens tournament we had won, I thought that might have pleased him. I sought out the club secretary Mary Charnock because the lads had not been paid, and it was only when she told me that I wasn't going to be paid that I twigged why Maurice had done his vanishing trick.

Eventually I tracked him down and demanded to know why I wasn't being paid, that I would decide which charity to give my money to and wasn't I the coach? Winning the competition hadn't just happened by accident.

We were alone in his office when, in real bookie style, he pulled out a huge wad of notes and said to me: 'You're money mad. You're always on about money.'

I tried to keep my cool and answered, 'No, Maurice, I'm not always on about money – only my own money.'

Knowing me the way he did and knowing my temperament he knew he could only push me so far.

I said: 'Look, Maurice, I don't really care what you think. Just put my money on the table and we'll say no more about it.'

With that, he peeled off four or five notes and hurled them to the floor. 'There you are, you money-grabbing little bastard.'

Believe it or not, I was still trying to keep cool. 'Let me offer you a bit of advice, Maurice,' I said as calmly as my seething temper would allow. 'Either you pick that up or you'll be joining it inside thirty seconds.' He made no move to do that so I repeated it very slowly: 'Maurice, friend or no friend, chairman or no chairman, pick that up. And don't ever repeat what you've just called me. I have never been money-grabbing, otherwise I wouldn't be working with you. You are not paying me a fortune and if you want me out, there are ways to do it. Now, I won't tell you again. Pick that money up.'

He was sitting behind his desk and he made no move so I leaned across and was going to yank him over the desk and make him pick up the money. But he grabbed hold of me and wouldn't let go, so – and I know I shouldn't have done it – I cracked him. He went toppling over the desk and the telephone shot up in the air and landed on top of him. Believe me, if the stories about trying to strangle him with the telephone wire were true, he would be dead by now.

I turned to go out of the office and he came running after me and said: 'I'm not afraid of you – I can fight, you know.'

'I'm glad to hear it,' I said, 'because if we ever start to really fight, I'll kill you.'

12

As I was leaving he put his arm around me and I felt like laughing out loud at the whole business. But I knew then that it was the end. That he had won. He had found a way to get me out.

He then went upstairs as if nothing had happened and even sat next to my wife Alice. He never said a word about what had gone on in the office. Talk about being cool . . . Maurice was a master.

I was hauled before the board of directors at their next meeting and was asked to resign. My cause wasn't helped by the fact that Maurice appeared with the best black eye I had ever seen – obviously my punch was a lot better than I thought.

I had done wrong. My defence was that, even if the rest of the board were going to allow Maurice to walk all over them, I wasn't going to let it happen to me. They decided that they could not allow a coach to go around punching a director and I had to go. Maurice had got his way. I was out of a job. It had definitely been a bad day at the office.

Although Maurice and I have crossed paths many times since that day, I never did find out what happened to those notes lying all over the floor. I hope they found a good home.

*

The parting of the ways was swift after that board meeting but the bitterness hasn't gone away even after all these years. I may be accused of being paranoid about the man and his ways, and perhaps some of the stories I have heard have been only for my benefit or to keep the pot boiling, because there's nothing some people like more than a good, festering row between two high-profile people who were once friends.

13

But, as we spent nearly ten years without getting back on speaking terms, I have to believe that there is some truth in the messages that have been passed down. For instance, it was during Maurice Lindsay's reign as chief executive that I lost my job on the BBC television commentary team. Now, I don't claim to have been the best commentator there has ever been but I had held the position for sixteen years and I think I did know a bit about the game. Word got back to me that there had been a phone call to the BBC – and it went a lot higher than rugby league producer Malcolm Kemp – from somebody in high authority inside the game suggesting that I was upsetting too many people in the sport and that I should be removed from the gantry.

I admit that, over the years I may have crossed swords with one or two folk along the way but I could think of nobody I had upset so much that they would bear a grudge big enough to try to have me sacked. Did I say nobody? Well, perhaps there was one. And when that was followed by more leaks that various clubs had been warned off employing me – again from somebody high up in the rugby league organisation – it did seem to go a bit deeper than simple paranoia.

Of course, since those dark, closing days at Wigan I have worked at other clubs and have become friends with so many good rugby league people who have appreciated what I had to offer – and on both sides of the Pennines, too, which is supposed to be the great divide within the game.

I am saddened as well as bitter about what happened between me and Maurice but I do not have any regrets. I did what I believed to be right at the time because I had to make a stand. And when he decided to step down in 1999 after what he described as 'twenty years' service to the game with barely a day off', I couldn't help but chuckle.

Maurice is not the retiring type and he was barely out of his Super League Europe office in Leeds before he was back at the helm of Wigan where it all really started. It was a move that confirmed every denied newspaper report that had appeared ever since it was announced that he was quitting his Super League position.

I have probably given the impression that I promoted Little Mo as my own personal albatross, *bête noire* or Private Enemy Number One, and that he was responsible for all the ills of the world of rugby league. And that is exactly how I felt for more than ten years after he saw me off from the biggest club in the world.

Well . . . was he all that bad? Even though for years we did not have a civil word to say to each other, I have to admire the way he succeeded in his first stint at Wigan after I had left and was out of his hair. I didn't like the way he treated me, though – I didn't like the way he took the credit for everything that happened without ever mentioning my name as the man who put all the ideas into his head.

While I was there Wigan went back to Wembley for the first time in many years and it was the start of big things for Maurice Lindsay. Then he turned on me and made sure that I was dumped out of the club. That still rankles more than anything else that has happened to me over the years. But you tend to mellow as you get older, don't you? After all, he did take me to the club and give me the opportunity to work for some of the best supporters in rugby league, and I am grateful for that. And he must have been doing something else right along the way. After his stint at Super League ended he was back at the club which had already honoured him by making him the only non-player in their Hall of Fame. The Wigan fans clearly think a lot of him and believe

15

he is the man to lead them into a golden age to go with their new JJB Stadium. Perhaps along the way he has learned from his mistakes – and it would be less than honest to say he hasn't made a few in those twenty years: his failure to delegate and desire to be a one-man band, his unilateral decision to give the Championship Trophy to Wigan, summer rugby, the Sky deal, and the dreaded mergers are all part of the Lindsay era.

But now he is back at Wigan at a time when the club needs somebody strong at the helm. This time he has to have the right people around him. The club's decline from stars of the golden age to a bunch of also-rans with a spanking new stadium but nothing in the trophy cabinet will bring a fresh challenge to Maurice Lindsay and I am fairly sure that, given his track record, he can turn things around.

We are again on speaking terms and have even enjoyed the occasional drink together – like I said, no feud can last forever – and I would like to think we can both let bygones be bygones. Who knows, maybe we could even work together again. After all, we managed quite well until that particularly bad day at the office.

TWO

Dives, dodges and other con jobs

I have been accused of pulling a few stunts in my time, and maybe that's true. But one of the proudest moments of my career was sullied for years by nods, winks and innuendo – suggestions that I had taken a dive at Wembley to get a fellow professional sent off. There were even accusations that, as I was waiting to be stretchered to the Wembley dressing-room, I winked at my assailant as he was ordered from the field.

Now, I have never denied that I have had a colourful career that included pulling the odd fast one or trying to con the referee once or twice, but even a scrum-half who is expected to know all the tricks of the trade has to know where to draw the line. And, for all those who passed judgement on me that day in 1971, I can tell you – they got it all wrong. I did not and never would take a dive to get a fellow player sent off. If

I had, does anybody think that Syd Hynes, who earned notoriety as the first man ever to be dismissed in a rugby league Cup final, would still be speaking to me? After all these years, we are still friends. So what really happened that afternoon when I was accused of playing to the galleries?

As rugby league fans of the day will remember, Leeds were red-hot favourites for the Cup and they felt they had only to turn up against a team of no-hopers from little Leigh to get their hands on the big prize. Well, things didn't turn out like that for a lot of reasons.

For a start, Leigh were no mugs. We had a team of talented youngsters mixed with some players of experience who were prepared to put their bodies on the line. We had already done the double over Leeds in the League that season and we had come through a tough semi-final against Huddersfield. So we were ready for the final – a lot better prepared, it seems, than the high-and-mighty Leeds.

You can picture the scene – Leeds can see the Cup slipping away . . . the upstarts from Leigh are running away with the Cup and are leading 17–2. Something has got to be done – and Syd is just the man to do it. It came as no great surprise to me that the Leeds centre was waiting for his chance to put Murphy's lights out. I spotted him coming but for once wasn't quick enough to do anything about it and, when he caught me on the temple, my lights did go out.

Anybody who asks me what happened next will have to settle for a vague recollection of being hauled aboard a stretcher. I had no idea that Syd had been sent off. And, as for winking at him on his way to the tunnel . . . well, that's just a handy myth to tag on to the colourful career of Alex Murphy. In fact, I was surprised that Syd had been sent packing. The referee was Billy Thompson and he and I had had our fair share of slanging matches over the years. In those days he was not the sort of referee that would go out of his way to do Alex Murphy any favours. Not long before Wembley he had been in charge of a Leigh game in which he had sent off one of our forwards, Dave Chisnall, a dismissal that obviously put the lad's Wembley place in jeopardy. I told him so – and added as a rider: 'If you get the Cup final I bet you won't have the balls to do the same at Wembley!'

Billy challenged me later saying: 'If I do get Wembley, you just let me get on with refereeing the game and we'll see if I am up to it.'

Well, here was his chance. A Leeds player, and a famous international at that, had flattened an opponent with an attack to the head. Would Billy, indeed, have the balls to send him off? I learned later that it wasn't quite as simple as that – Billy had consulted the touch judge and asked the inevitable question: 'Was it a sending-off offence?' When he got the nod, off went Syd.

I admit I may have rolled about a bit and I am a better actor than most but, according to some judges that day – many of them from more than sixty yards away – I should have got an Oscar instead of a Cup final medal. In the meantime, I was being stretchered to the dressing-room where I was examined by an independent doctor. The next thing I remember is being woken up in the bath and being told that I was wanted back out on the pitch to collect the Cup. The doctor said I was in no fit state to get dressed because I had been badly concussed. However, they did manage to patch me up and I did go back out there for the grand finale . . .

Leigh had won the Cup 24–7 and I was voted Man of the Match and picked up the Lance Todd Trophy. And all those people who say I conned referee Billy Thompson cannot explain how I also managed to con rugby league's disciplinary committee who, after studying film evidence of the incident, dished out a six-match ban on Syd Hynes.

As I have said, there are certain things a player will do outside the laws of the game to win a match and I have probably tried most of them in my time, but taking a dive to get an opponent sent off isn't one of them. Syd Hynes knows that and so does Billy Thompson. My conscience is clear.

*

All this doesn't mean to say that I was always wearing a halo, even during my time as a Saint, and it was during an earlier trip to Wembley – for a Cup final against the old enemy, Wigan – that I gathered the unwelcome label of Cheat. But, at the risk of being branded again – this time as a poor, sad individual feeling sorry for himself and pleading he was misunderstood – I believe that, at the time, I was using the rules but was not doing anything anybody else would not have done. I just thought of it first.

There are certain times when gamesmanship is as big a part of a rugby match as the accepted skills and strengths. It may not be right or gentlemanly but it has helped to win many a match. And nobody ever suggested that rugby league was supposed to be gentlemanly!

If pulling the odd trick or two could mean the difference between a few extra bob to keep the family and a week of being hard up and explaining to workmates how we managed to lose a certain match then I would be among the first in line to try it. Remember, in those days, even the top rugby league players were part-timers.

It was in that climate that I soon learned that not only was a bit of rule-bending gamesmanship accepted, it was actually expected from me. Such an occasion was the 1966 Challenge Cup final, St Helens v. Wigan. Those were the days when possession was nine-tenths of the rugby league law and hookers were key figures in the game. It so happened that Saints had one of the best in Bill Sayer, who had been sold to the club by Wigan to make way for a talented up-and-coming youngster called Colin Clarke. However, it happened that Clarke had been suspended for the final so Wigan were having to field their second choice, Bill Woosey. It did not take a genius to work out that, if it came to head-to-heads, our Bill would beat their Bill hands down. Sayer was one of the old-fashioned hookers who took a great pride in his art. If I threw three balls into the tunnel at once he would get the lot. Up against him was a mere novice, so possession from the scrum was not going to be a problem.

There have been many rule changes over the years and I am convinced – and so are a lot of other people – that I was responsible for at least one of them after that 1966 Cup final. In the 1960s a penalty kick that found touch was not, as today, followed by a tap where the victims retained possession. Instead, there would be a scrum-down ten yards in from where the ball crossed the touchline.

As we were walking up the Wembley tunnel I fired the first bullets in the nerve war that goes with every major match. I turned to Bill Sayer and said, loud enough for Wigan skipper Eric Ashton to hear: 'Don't forget to bring that bucket of cold water with you.'

A puzzled Ashton clearly wondered what I was talking about, so I explained: 'Sayer will be striking for the ball so fast his foot will be red-hot – the water will cool him down.'

Okay, so it was only a silly remark designed to wind up the opposition, but it was enough to set the wheels in motion for what was to turn out to be one of the most one-sided Wembley Cup finals ever played. Part Two of the plan was to use, bend or at least make the most of the rules.

Whenever Wigan were in possession and on the point of building what could have been a threatening attack, it just so happened that I might perhaps wander offside, conceding the penalty. Wigan would duly kick for touch, the team would scrum down and, true to form, Sayer would shovel the ball out on our side and the whole Wigan attack would collapse in a heap.

It became embarrassing to the point where Eric knew that kicking for touch was more of a disadvantage. Saints strolled to a comfortable 21–2 win and the rugby league hierarchy had to have a rethink about the rules. Was I cheating – or just playing to the rules as they were? The game's bosses obviously thought I had found a loophole in the laws and promptly changed the punishment for the crime of being caught offside.

Now that the art of hooking has gone completely from the modern game and the rules about scrummaging don't mean much, I suppose I was only a temporary nuisance to the rule-makers.

Far more damaging to the game was another alteration for which I was partly responsible – but here the blame lies with the people who made the decision to devalue the drop-goal to one point. Drop-goal kicking is a skill that takes hours of practice to perfect. I remember my first coach, Jim Sullivan, telling me that the drop-goal – then worth two points (a try was three in those days) – could have a devastating effect on the opposition. When you seemed to have been attacking for ever without any signs of breaking through, a drop-goal brought a whole new pattern to the game as well as two points. If I could drop four a game, that was eight points – and it would need three tries to beat it.

Today, with the drop-goal at one point and the try at four, one of the major skills of the game has been devalued so much that we hardly ever see it.

I can still feel the thrill of watching the ball soar over the posts from forty-five yards out, hearing the crowd going wild at this total break-up in the pattern of play that was becoming sterile. By halving the value of the drop-goal, the game's rulers have more or less taken it out of the system – a bit like penalising a soccer club for having a player who can score direct from a corner or a David Beckham who can bend the ball around the wall. Without them the game would suffer as a spectacle – as rugby league has done.

*

Getting on well with a referee could always tip the balance just when you needed it. Most of the refs knew I was the archetypal scrum-half with a lot to say, trying to run the game from the start. But they and I knew exactly how far to go. It was all about man-management. The top referee of his time was the man we all called the Sergeant Major – Eric Clay from Castleford. He wouldn't stand any nonsense and you knew that if you overstepped the mark the result was an early bath. But at least you could speak to him so I was always tempted to find out just how far I could go.

There was one of the Rugby League Cup's big occasions when a word in the ear of the Sergeant Major was enough to turn defeat into a famous victory and earn a local club steward a punch on the nose! Hull Kingston Rovers had played St Helens off the park and were heading for a famous victory. The home crowds were streaming towards the exits of Knowsley Road on their way home or to the local pub to drown their sorrows. We had hammered away at the Hull KR line but were getting nowhere. It was deep into injury time at the end of the match. As another attack ground to a halt, I had a quick word with Mr Clay, asking him how long there was to play. The usual response would have been that that was for him to know and for me to guess. In the days before timekeepers and hooters, the referee was the sole judge of eighty minutes. 'There are only seconds to go,' he told me, and I knew then that at the next tackle he would blow his whistle and Saints would be on their way out of the Cup. There was no time for me to get the ball along the line and out to the wings – the usual route to a try when laying siege to the opposition line. So, as a last, desperate ploy I hoisted a towering up-and-under towards the Hull KR posts. The full-back suddenly got an attack of the jitters and somehow managed to spill the ball. I followed up and pounced on it, touching down for the winning try. Sounds simple, doesn't it? But others were far from convinced – including half my own team and the referee in charge. I made a big thing about having got the winning touchdown and I am sure that helped.

Eric Clay clearly knew that he had given me a vital piece of information that amounted to an unfair advantage so, instead of immediately awarding the try, he consulted his touch judges desperately trying, I think, to find a reason to disallow it. But it was good and the score stood. Hull Kingston, who had been far and away the better team, were out of the Cup.

Big Frank Foster, their massive forward, was furious – he was convinced it was no try. 'Check it in the papers tomorrow, Frank, you'll see it was a try,' I told him. It wasn't the only time I rubbed the big guy up the wrong way and I felt a bit sorry for him.

Not as sorry, though, as I did for the steward of the local labour club. By the end of the match many of his regulars were already queuing up to drown their sorrows, muttering tales of 'being let down' and 'not getting to Wembley this year'. In an attempt to cheer up the place, the steward explained, 'But they've won – Murphy scored a try in the last minute to win the match.' Nobody believed him – and some even accused him of taking the piss. One supporter who had suffered seventy-nine minutes of the game took it on himself to vent his anger on the landlord, by taking a swing at the unfortunate bearer of the good news!

*

Pulling a fast one or working a flanker may have been part of the game but it did not always work out for the best. However, I never thought I would see the day when one of my best friends would be behind the move to get me sent off.

Once again it was a Wigan–St Helens match and again it was daggers drawn between the two arch-rivals. I had been chosen to play at stand-off instead of my normal scrum-half position, and facing me in the Wigan number 6 jersey was a good friend Michael Sullivan. Sullivan, it so happened, was a natural winger who had never played stand-off before – which meant that he could be there for one thing only: to keep an eye on Murphy and make sure I didn't do any damage.

It was only a matter of time before we clashed – you don't have any friends in opposition jerseys for eighty minutes – and true to form there was a flare-up. Sullivan knew exactly how I would react when, after a tackle, he threw the ball in my face. I didn't let him down: there was a flurry of punches and, when it was all sorted out, there was the referee pointing to the dressing-rooms. We had both been sent off.

As we left the field, the Wigan captain – that gentleman among players, Eric Ashton, who would never stoop so low as to try anything underhand – said: 'Well done, Sully, we'll manage without you, but they won't be able to get by without *him*.'

And so it turned out. Wigan won the match. They had got one over on Saints in general and me in particular. I had to hold my hands up and admit it.

But that was not the end of the matter. It was only afterwards that I learned that the Saints board were not happy with yours truly, that they blamed me for rising to the bait. Nobody tried to explain why they had picked me at stand-off in the first place and so set up the inevitable collision. It was a backhanded compliment, I suppose. No opposing team would go to the trouble of trying to get a poor player sent off, would they?

I have been booed on most grounds in rugby league but I knew I had talent and nobody could ever accuse me of not going out to entertain. I have lost count of the number of times I left grounds and overheard supporters or club officials saying: 'That Murphy's a real bastard – but I wish he played for us.'

Those memories provide more than enough evidence to know that my playing career was a success – and I didn't do too badly as a coach later in life, either.

THREE

School of hard knocks and ballet dancers

The old saying about the futility of banging your head against a brick wall was obviously lost on the rugby players at St Austin's School in St Helens. It did them the power of good. It was all the brainwave of one of the biggest influences in my young sporting life, the school's headmaster Gerry Landers. The three men who shaped my future both inside and outside the rugby ground were my father, Gerry Landers and the greatest rugby legend of them all, Jim Sullivan.

I was born at 25 Sunbury Street in the Thatto Heath area of St Helens on 22 April 1939, the youngest of the family. I had one older brother, Billy, and three sisters, Annie, Nellie and Jean. My father James had a spell playing for Warrington but I never got to find out how good he was. He worked as a stoker of the boilers at the local mental hospital and my mother Sally worked at Pilkington's glassworks in the town.

They earned just enough to keep a family of our size – we were never rich.

I suppose it was my father's job that taught me the value of being quick off the mark. In those days in the late 1940s mental hospitals were regarded as frightening places full of bad men, and a kid of ten would believe exactly what he was told. One of my jobs was to take my dad's dinner up to him at the hospital. I was always wary and spent most of my time on the 500-yard road up to the hospital scouring the bushes on the look-out for patients. I can tell you – as soon as I saw one I was off like a shot. My dad's dinner may have been spilled a few times but he never got it cold!

With my dad having played rugby at Warrington and brother Billy a highly talented table-tennis player (he had been known to take on the touring professionals and beat them in exhibition matches) I suppose I had a head start in the sporting sense.

Billy, a pit worker, was one of the best table-tennis players in Lancashire and one of the first, I believe, to use the penholder grip. I remember one occasion when Billy, who would have been about twenty at the time, reached the final of a major championship and we all got on the bus to Peasey Cross to go and watch him play. We got there a bit early and were greeted by Billy who offered to take Dad for a pint. He was so shocked that my brother drank that he hauled him off home and my brother did not play in the final.

Billy was talented at cricket, football and rugby but he ended up doing none of them. I thought – what a waste of talent. And so did my dad. He was worried that I might also waste what talent I had and, although he encouraged me and wanted me to get on in the game, it was really my first headmaster Gerry Landers who set me on the road to a career in rugby league.

I went to St Austin's – a local school of fewer than a hundred pupils which also produced another rugby league star, Austin Rhodes. I suppose I was never destined to be an academic because I was far too interested in sport and because of that I let other things slide. But Gerry Landers spotted that I had something and I owe him so much for getting me started at such an early age.

I must have been about eleven years old when he first took me to one side and, in front of the rest of the lads in the playground, tried to explain to me that rugby was like dancing! I mean – what self-respecting eleven-year-old rugby player would associate his favourite sport with dancing? He explained by demonstrating how to pass the ball. One-two-three to the right, one-two-three to the left. And he kept me at it for up to an hour at a time while all my mates stood around laughing!

During all that time I never actually got my hands on a rugby ball – it was all down to imagination. I can tell you – it's embarrassing to be called a 'big Jessie, ballet dancer' when you're that age. But, although I didn't appreciate it at the time, it became a valuable weapon in later years when I was able to pass the ball off the ground, both ways.

The ballet-style passing lessons were not the head's only idea of how to train for important matches; there was always the stone wall that surrounded the playing-field. Gerry Landers knew that we would have to come up against much bigger and stronger lads, so he devised a plan to get the ball from the scrum – and it involved pushing into a stone wall. These days scrums are predictable and only rugby union forwards know what a scrum machine is for, but in my schooldays every ball had to be fought for and every scrum was a battle for possession. To increase our chances I, along with the six forwards, would be asked to go to the top of the field and form a pack – and start pushing against a stone wall. I would put the ball into the scrum, and the hooker, a lad called Pat Feeny, would heel it out as quickly as he could.

Unfortunately for his front-row partner Tony Allcock, the head was a stickler for proper scrummaging. He knew that, unlike the wall, the opposition would be pushing back. Poor Tony, a chubby lad – every team had to have one – had a habit of sticking his backside out of the scrum and, whenever he did, it was quickly returned by a sharp crack from the headmaster's stick which he kept hidden behind his back. It was enough to make any kid push harder even against a wall. It's a good thing we never had the strength to push the wall over – there was a 150-foot drop the other side!

But the ballet-dancing-cum-passing lessons, and the beating-your-head-against-the-wall sessions must have worked: we went on to reach the final of the Daily Dispatch Shield – the big schools trophy in those days.

Although I played rugby every chance I got, it was not my only sport. I liked football too and even had trials for Everton as a kid. My first serious injury came from an impromptu schoolyard soccer match. I was just as cocky on a football pitch as I was on a rugby field, always with an eye to do something smart. Not everybody appreciated it, so when I trapped the ball a lad called Frankie Elliott didn't stand on ceremony. Instead, he stood on my ankle – in his bloody great clogs!

I went home for lunch complaining of a sore and swollen ankle but my dad, thinking I was only trying to skip lessons, ordered me back to school. It was only at the end of the afternoon that I was allowed to go to hospital – to be told that my ankle was broken.

That incident was almost as painful as the time I was nearly banned from playing rugby and football because of a boil on my neck! I had been chosen for two town team trial matches the following morning – the football team at ten o'clock and the rugby team three hours later. But I reckoned without my mother. She took one look at the state of my neck and said: 'You're going nowhere with that unless you let me lance it.' If you think breaking an ankle is sore, or getting a clout from the biggest, roughest rugby player in Christendom is painful, believe me they have nothing on a bread poultice and a boil-lancing. It was agony! But it was worth it – I made it to the trials and into both teams the next day.

Even so, I never had the 'feel' for soccer that I had for rugby. Even when I got the trial for Everton it was only because it was something to do while there was no rugby match on. When I told them I couldn't wait to get back to playing rugby they said I must be mad. Maybe . . . but football was too timid for me.

I enjoyed the matches on the local park – married men against single men – where we had to wait for the married men to come out of the pub before we could start. Among the players kept waiting for a game was a certain Bill Foulkes who went on to Manchester United. We knew he would do well – he was the only one with the proper kit!

Before I left school I had the privilege of playing against and alongside the best schoolboy rugby player I had ever seen – Jackie Edwards, the father of record-breaking London Broncos and former Wigan and Bradford scrum-half Shaun Edwards. Although I signed Shaun for Wigan at his home at midnight on his seventeenth birthday – October 1982 – and believe that he is and has been one of the finest talents in the modern game, I have to say that I think Jackie was an even better player as a kid. Jackie and I could both play in two positions, stand-off or scrum-half. It could be argued that he was the best in Wigan and I was the best in St Helens, so when Wigan played St Helens, we were lined up opposite each other. When we played for Lancashire, on the other hand, we were partners. Not equal partners as it turned out, since Jackie got preferential treatment when it came to travelling with the county team up to far-off Cumberland. There were no motorways or high-powered superbuses in those days, just the bone-rattling charabanc that took about six hours to get to places like Workington or Whitehaven. Not for Jackie, though: he couldn't go by team bus because he suffered from travel sickness so he went all the way by train. He would arrive as fresh as a daisy while the rest of us were worn out and covered with bumps and bruises before we even kicked off!

Rivals as only Wiganers and St Helens can be, we were a team on the field for Lancashire and we promised each other that when we signed professional forms – and there was never any doubt that we would – we would stick together and sign for the same club. Well, so much for promises! The next thing I hear is that Warrington have whipped Jackie off to Blackpool, made him an offer he couldn't refuse – a thousand quid, I was led to believe – and signed him on professional forms. I left school at the age of fifteen, signed for hometown St Helens on my sixteenth birthday and began what for me has been a wonderful life in rugby league that has allowed me to travel to Australia to represent my country, play in Challenge Cup finals and Test matches at Wembley, play with and coach some of the game's finest players, collect an OBE and spend forty years among some of sport's finest. And if I could lay the credit at the feet of one man, it would be the all-time great of the 1930s through to the 1950s – I may have mentioned him before – Jim Sullivan.

FOUR

Jim, you'll get the little lad killed!

With Jackie Edwards off to Warrington, the chances of Lancashire's two best schoolboy half-backs linking up and forming a partnership to frighten the life out of the rest of rugby league – he was the king of Wigan and I was the best in St Helens – had disappeared.

So it was off to hometown St Helens to join my first professional club and to team up with the man who was to shape my rugby life. I had been training with St Helens since I was fourteen so I already knew Jim Sullivan and he knew about me. In fact, we came close to falling out the very first time we met. He threw me a pair of running spikes – I had never seen any before – and told me to go to the track which ran alongside the training ground.

Running alongside in a fifty-yard sprint were Frank Carlton, the first-team winger and one of the fastest men in the country. Beside him was Alec Davis, another sprinter, and Eric Ledger who was a bit smart as well. Over a fifty-yard sprint I came in trailing by about twenty yards! It was embarrassing and I was still a schoolboy. I suppose it should have knocked some of the cockiness of youth out of me but it didn't.

'I'm not doing that again,' I told the coach. 'Did you see it? I was miles behind.'

Jim Sullivan put his arm round my shoulder and said: 'Let's see how far behind you are in a couple of years' time.' From that moment on, he treated me like a son – and it was like having a second dad.

When the time came for me to sign professional forms for St Helens I still wasn't sure. After all, my last game as an amateur was in a Cup final and I had scored three tries. I knew the game had been watched by a lot of club scouts and I had played well enough to get people talking. But Harry Cooke, the chairman of St Helens and another man who had a big influence on my life, was ready to beat off any challengers for my signature. He took me upstairs and then sent for my dad. The idea was to sign me at midnight on my sixteenth birthday so they smuggled me off to the house of one of the directors, Joe Harrison, and there I stayed until midnight when I duly signed professional forms. And I think I can safely say I didn't do it for the signing-on fee – I was paid the princely sum of eighty pounds. Actually, it was only forty quid because I had already received forty pounds in an illegal payment made when I was still fifteen. But that midnight signing in 1955 was the first step in my career in what I still believe to be the greatest game in the world.

Mind you, if a certain lady had had her way I might never have got off the training ground. I was only a titch and when I came to have the official publicity photograph taken, I sat on a bench and my feet hardly reached the ground. Mrs

Sullivan, the coach's wife, saw me and turned to her husband. 'You're not letting him play rugby – you'll get the little lad killed,' she told him.

'Don't worry,' was his reply, 'there'll be a few around who get killed before he does.'

Whether she was happy with that I never knew, but perhaps it was partly her concern that caused Jim to treat me the way he did. Even though he had time for everybody and he had to handle some of the world's greatest players, I felt that working with Jim Sullivan was like having my own private coach.

It would be wrong, though, to think that it was sweetness and light all the time between us and, in fact, I was still only sixteen when I made my first transfer request. Saints had been flying in the Challenge Cup and were on the way to Wembley but there were still a few League games to play so, in order to protect the players who would be turning out in the Cup final, the club decided to field a scratch team for a midweek match against Whitehaven at Knowsley Road. There was only one recognised first-teamer in the side which was packed with young hopefuls like myself. I loved it and I knew that I had had a good game – so much so that I thought I was better than everybody else at the club. I felt I should stay in the first team even though I knew I was only there in the first place because there was a fixture congestion and Sullivan was experimenting. I'd scored a try, made a couple of others and we whipped the Cumbrians in fine style. To my mind – young and enthusiastic as I was – I had done more than enough to justify another run-out in the team at the next game.

Not only did that fail to happen, but Jim Sullivan spent an age pointing out all my faults and I was actually dropped from the 'A' team. I went home and told my dad I was going to ask for a move. So he took me along to see Sullivan to tell him that I wasn't very happy and would like a transfer.

Jim took my father to one side and had a quiet word in his ear, the gist of which was: 'Mr Murphy, he's a cocky little so-and-so but you let me look after the little fella and I promise you I will see to it that he gets a fair deal. He will get his chance when I think he is ready.'

That was good enough for my father, who gave me a crack round the ear and told me to knuckle down and do as I was told.

If it was good enough for my dad then it had to be good enough for me so I did exactly that and I was a regular in the first team when I was seventeen years old. By that time Jim Sullivan had coached me in so many things, including the drop-goal – even teaching me how to drop a goal when facing the wrong way.

I knuckled down to training and listened to his advice. I was often at the ground two hours before everybody else and was always the last away – usually after some extra training alongside Vince Karalius. It was Sullivan who kept me out of so many scrapes with his sound advice: 'He's a bit slow, that one, Spud, run away from him,' – or – 'He's a big lad so keep away from him or he could do you some damage.'

It didn't always work and I still managed to get into trouble of my own making. I suppose it was that cockiness and refusal to take a backward step that got me into trouble. But Sullivan's advice was usually sound and when I listened I managed to keep out of hot water. A butcher by trade, he was a convert to the game having come up from the Welsh valleys. He had the appearance of a gentleman farmer and he always liked to make sure he was doing what was best for his players. Whenever we travelled to away games, especially up into Cumberland, we would stop off at the best hotels.

He was a strict but very kind man and if there was ever anybody in my life with whom I would gladly spend time on a desert island it would be Jim Sullivan. He made me feel good from the start. I remember asking him to tell me what he thought was the difference between a good player and a great player. He stretched out his arm and said: 'This is the difference. They can either catch you or you get away by only as much as a yard but that yard makes all the difference. A good player can be kept quiet for eighty minutes in a match. A great player can only be kept quiet for seventy-nine and in that extra minute he will destroy you. You have only to think you have kept him buttoned up, done a good day's work and are ready to pat yourself on the back when – zip, he's done you. Seventy-nine minutes spent doing nothing, one minute spent winning the game. That's a great player for you, Spud.' And he stretched out his arm again to show that the yard between being caught and being nailed was all it took.

As I have said, he had some of the world's great players under his wing and one of the best of them all was the legendary South African Tom van Vollenhoven. Here again, we did not get off to the best of starts.

The story had gone round that Tom, who had never played a game of rugby league in his life but was a Springbok rugby union international, had been paid eight thousand pounds to join Saints. Now eight grand in those days was a whole lot of money for an untried winger so I was a bit surprised when, on the first day of training, Jim Sullivan took me to one side and said: 'Spud, I want you to go out there and show Voll how to play the ball.'

I looked at him blankly for a second and then said: 'Am I getting this right? You want me to show him how to play the ball? I signed for this club for eighty quid and he has signed for eight thousand – I think for that kind of money he can teach himself how to play the bloody ball!'

It was the sort of cocky remark Jim Sullivan had come to expect from me but he hardly turned a hair except to remind me that I and the rest of the lads would be earning a lot more winning pay-packets with him in the team than without him. And he hadn't even seen him play.

Once again, it turned out Sullivan was right. As soon as I set eyes on the South African, I thought – what an athlete! Small head, powerful body and strong legs, he was built for rugby league.

I had seen and played against the finest try-scoring winger there has ever been – the Austalian, Brian Bevan. Bald, bony and bandy-legged he looked more like Steptoe's horse than a rugby player, but all you had to do was to put the ball in his hands and watch him go.

Vollenhoven was never going to match the Australian in scoring tries but he was to become a Saints legend. Like most converts from rugby union, he was a bit slow to make the change from what was an amateur code to playing for money – and *winning* money in particular. In one of his early games he played against Leeds. Their team included a winger called Pat Quinn who was an ex-England rugby union player who was no mug. He came face to face with Vollenhoven, chipped the ball over his head and went round him to re-gather. When we got into the dressing-room, Sullivan collared Vollenhoven about the incident. 'I hope that's the last time I ever see you do that!'

In all innocence, Vollenhoven said: 'What do you mean?'

'If anybody ever chips the ball over you again I want to see you put them in the stand!'

Vollenhoven was a quick learner. Although Quinn scored a try in their first meeting, when he tried it again in the last match of the season, he duly made his visit to the stand!

Although Sullivan was a great coach and, in my eyes, a great man, he didn't win every battle – although he came closer than anybody to making the biggest scoop in rugby league history, such were his persuasive powers.

At the time St Helens were determined to build a world-class side, a team of players who would become the envy of every club from Sydney northwards. And it was thanks to Sullivan that they came within a whisker of signing the greatest stand-off half Wales had ever produced: the legendary Cliff Morgan.

Cliff was in the Saints dressing-room pondering over a six-thousand-pound signing-on fee and fellow Welshman Sullivan had all but persuaded the great man to make the change which, in those days, was like burning all your bridges – even becoming an outcast in your own land, disowned by your fans and shunned by friends. For a rugby union player of the calibre of Cliff Morgan to switch codes – 'defect' was the word they used, as though you had betrayed your country – was unthinkable.

Well, he did think about it – long and hard – before turning it down. And, to this day, I believe that, despite rugby union's amateur status, its upper-class, fair-play image, Cliff got a matching six-thousand-pound offer to stay in rugby union.

Yes, Cliff may have been the one that got away, but Jim Sullivan was still the greatest man I ever met in the game of rugby. He was a coach forty years ahead of his time and I am sad that he didn't live long enough to see the fruits of his labours with that 'cocky little so-and-so' he took under his wing. I believe he would have said that I made a lot of use of that eightieth minute and the yard that separated the good players from the greats.

FIVE

Minders, assassins and other forms of wildlife

I was not long into my professional career when I learned that there were certain no-go areas on a rugby league field for a player standing only five foot nine with his boots on. Anywhere within the boundaries of a scrum was one such zone.

Nowadays, when an international coach can choose a team that expects somebody with the looks, the skills and the size of Henry Paul to stick his head in the front row of a scrum, it is a sure sign that life in the game has changed. Henry Paul, one of the modern game's leading talents whether it is at stand-off or at full-back, was hooker in the New Zealand team for the trans-Tasman Test series against Australia in 1998 after making a name for himself as Wigan's match-winning stand-off – a position he then made his own at Bradford Bulls.

In the late 1950s you would not get any self-respecting half-back going anywhere near a scrum – at least not twice. It was bad enough standing alongside the twelve-man wars of attrition just to put the ball in the tunnel without encroaching on their space. And it was *their* space – it belonged to the forwards . . . big, hard, unfeeling men who protected their positions of power and scorned the fancy-dan backs, the brylcreem boys of the game.

I learned just how much of a forbidden territory the twelve square yards or so around the scrum was during a game at Halifax. We were up against a formidable Yorkshire pack that included the great Jack Wilkinson, a man of massive proportions who was reputed to eat scrum-halves alive and spit out the pieces.

Not that Saints were short of big, rough-and-ready forwards either but, as I said, that was their territory and they were welcome to it. Scrums in those days were competitive. All right, so they were a bit of a mess with legs and arms – especially a hooker's loose-arm getting in the way of a decent scrum-feed – but there was an element of surprise about the result. That doesn't happen today, when the scrum-half feeds the loose-forward who picks it up without anybody getting a foot to it – but that's another story.

This was one of those occasions that got the rugby league scrum its bad name – the forwards, refusing to give an inch, pushed and shoved and grunted their way into an unholy mess and managed to turn the scrum round completely. And somewhere among all that sweating beef was a rugby ball. Somehow I found myself on the wrong side of the heaving mass and I was trying to reach into the scrum to get the ball out while the two sets of forwards were otherwise engaged. I found myself staring into the face of the snarling Jack

Wilkinson and I believe there was genuine hate in his eyes when he said: 'Get back round the other side, you little bastard – or I'll boot you back over this scrum.'

He would have done, as well, but I had been warned and it was foolish to ignore a warning from one of the most fearsome forwards in the game.

I promised myself to steer well clear of front-row forwards and never put my head into a scrum again. You do not mix with the sort of people who can seriously damage your health.

But, even keeping out of the way of scrums did not necessarily mean that I was out of danger. I can remember many occasions when, walking down the tunnel, I have heard opposition coaches tell their hit-men to 'get rid of Murphy'. Such instructions would not be tolerated these days and would be frowned upon if they ever reached the ears of the people in charge of the game, but you have to remember that rugby league in those days was a game for part-time profes-sionals and the difference between winning and losing meant a weight difference in the pay-packets. Today, in contrast, the contract system allows some players to pick up thousands of pounds without ever pulling on a pair of boots. In the old days we had to earn every extra pound the hard way.

So it should come as no surprise that little blokes like me needed a minder. And for much of my career I had the best: one Vincent Karalius, the man the Australians dubbed the Wild Bull of the Pampas. A scrap-metal dealer with hands like shovels, Karalius was like a minesweeper in front of me. Not only did he look after me, he 'looked after' the opposition as well. A quiet word in Vinty's ear was enough to make sure that I was not unwisely or unfairly treated by any of the opposition's hard men during the eighty minutes – life was a whole lot easier with him around.

Vince is one man who sticks in my mind when the students of the modern game start ranting on about how much fitter and faster today's full-time players are. Believe me, the man from Widnes was fit. He ran the fourteen miles to and from training – after putting in a day's work at the scrapyard – and he would be the last one away from the training ground. He trained as hard and as often as any of today's players. He was a magnificent athlete.

Another player whom it was always better to have on your side was Duggie Greenall. Duggie was not the world's best centre but when people talk about today's big-hits and king-hits, it is fairly obvious that they have never been tackled by Greenall. He had such a reputation for putting the opposition on to stretchers that it was rumoured he had plaster-of-Paris wrapped around his forearm to make sure that when he hit somebody they stayed hit. But Duggie needed no such extra help to carry out what he saw as his duty to the team and his pay-packet.

I remember one particular game at Oldham in the days when the Watersheddings, now gone and almost forgotten after a century as the home of some of the game's greats, was a rugby league fortress. Hardly any visiting teams ever won there and we went along as underdogs.

Oldham were a strong and powerful team with a half-back as good as I was and a hooker who was better than most, Jack Keith. Jim Sullivan's pre-match instructions won't be found in any modern-day coaching manuals and they're not something anybody would boast about. He simply said: 'I don't want to see that man Keith on the field at the end of the game.' Now, to Duggie, that meant only one thing – see him off on a stretcher!

It took all of eight minutes for the demon Duggie to strike

and for the Oldham hooker to be carried off, never to return. From then on, St Helens had no trouble, Duggie had done his job and the win bonus was on its way into our pay-packets and not theirs.

Feeling brave, I challenged Greenall about it. I asked: 'Why do you do that, Duggie?'

He looked puzzled. 'Do what?'

'You know, go around flattening people with stiff-arm tackles and getting them carried off.'

He said: 'Because I am a professional, I play for money, I play to win.'

That struck home but I stood my ground and said: 'But I am a professional. I play to win. What's the difference?'

He looked at me as though I had just dropped in from another planet. 'The difference between us, Spud, is that if that had been my mother out there in the opposition jersey, she would have ended up the same way.'

Duggie was clearly pointing out that he would go to any lengths to collect his bonus. I remembered never to ask him any more questions about the game in case I did not like the answers.

In those days, rugby league had a reputation among the rest of the country as a game for hooligans, played by hooligans and watched by hooligans. There were no half-measures in the condemnation by the chattering classes who firmly believed that it was all Eddie Waring, up-and-unders and whippets. But it was also a game of great skill that could pull in huge crowds – thirty thousand for a Wigan–Saints derby was not unusual – and when you consider that the players were part-timers, we certainly gave value for money.

That's not to say that we were forelock-tugging slaves all the time. There was the occasion when I thought I had played my last match for St Helens after I was told that I would be playing in the centre in a crucial game. I challenged the chairman, Harry Cook, pointing out that I had played regularly at scrum-half for Great Britain; and I had played stand-off for the national side.

But he interrupted: 'And you'll soon be good enough to play centre for Great Britain as well.'

I was having none of that: 'If you move me out any further I might as well be sitting in the bloody stand.' And I walked out. It was the beginning of the end.

So it was that stubborn streak on both sides that led to my departure from Saints, one of the biggest clubs in the game. And it was only months later when I bumped into one of the Saints directors that I discovered what was behind it all.

Like the rest of the rugby league clubs, Saints had the normal board of directors made up of local businessmen such as solicitors and shopkeepers – people who wanted to put something into the club without having millions of pounds to invest to chase their dream. But in reality they were ruled by the chairman, Harry Cook, and the secretary, Basil Lowe. If you wanted to talk business, you dealt with them; the rest of the board were there to be seen and not heard. It was a situation that led to my departure from the club I worshipped and into the job I came to love most of all throughout my career . . . at small-town Leigh.

There was a time when I would have crawled on all fours over broken glass to play for St Helens but there comes a stage when even such devoted loyalty passes breaking point and you have to move on. My dispute at St Helens over which position I played for the club was the point of no return.

It was after I was instructed by Harry Cook that I would

be playing in the centre and I told him I didn't like that idea one bit. I was Great Britain's number-one scrum-half; I liked to think I was as good a stand-off as the next man. But centre? No way . . . I liked to be close to the action.

At that time, Saints had brought in Tommy Bishop who was to become a Great Britain regular so they obviously felt that if Murphy threw a wobbly they would have the cover they needed. I suppose in a roundabout way they were paying me a compliment, but I didn't see it like that. As far as I was concerned I was scrum-half – the best there was – and centre was no place for me.

So I said: 'I'm sorry – but I am *not* playing in the centre.'

But, of course, I did. It was against Wakefield Trinity and I was given the job of marking the great Neil Fox – all sixteen-stone-plus of him. And me, by comparison, a twelve-and-a-half-stone midget. I had the greatest respect for Fox, who later went on to be rugby league's record points-scorer and a fellow member of the game's Hall of Fame. But then he was neither of those things – he was simply the famous Neil Fox.

'Don't worry about his reputation, or his size,' I was told. 'Just get stuck into him.' It was as though the chairman believed I had some magic wand that I only had to wave to make Fox disappear. 'Besides, you will play where we pick you – not where you decide you want to play.'

I got through that match with my health and reputation intact but as players in the centre position got about one pass every three weeks I can't say I enjoyed the experience. So I made my stand. I was told that if I didn't like it I would have to lump it and I would be banned from the club. That stunned me so I offered to play in the second team in an attempt to regain my place at scrum-half. But that wasn't good enough for them. I was told to stay away from the ground and ended up training with the local Pilkington's amateur club.

I went to Basil Lowe in an effort to settle the dispute – after all, he was the club secretary and I had no wish to be banned from my hometown club because of a disagreement over the position I would play in the team.

'I'll tell the board you want to talk to them,' was the nearest to an acknowledgement I ever got that there was actually something to talk about, but he came back to me with the message that the directors did not want to discuss the matter with me. It looked as though my days at Knowsley Road were over.

And so they were. But even that wasn't straightforward. It turned out that Saints were quite prepared to sell me – so long as it was to somewhere far, far away – like Australia. In fact, a fee of eight thousand pounds was agreed between Saints and North Sydney and I was on the brink of making the trip Down Under. But then my wife Alice and I talked about it and we came to the conclusion that it wasn't for us. Why should we have to leave our friends and families and travel nearly twelve thousand miles just to suit them?

So I stuck it out and was left out of the game for twelve months. I was at my wits' end and it wasn't until Leigh came along that I saw a way back into the game I loved. Saints had hurt me badly and my own stubborn streak had not helped the situation. I could be as awkward and as bloody-minded as the next man.

It was not until I had long left Saints behind that I learned the full story. It happened after a round of golf when I bumped into a Saints director, Sam Hall, in the carpark. He came over to me and started to ask me if I had any regrets about leaving Saints, telling me how stupid I was not to have listened to what the board had to say. I explained that I had tried to speak to the board and they had turned me down flat.

'Where did you get that idea – who told you that?' he asked.

'Basil Lowe.'

It was only then that I learned that as a so-called peacemaker, the Saints secretary had played a double bluff that hadn't worked and he wasn't going to admit it. It seemed that Harry Cook, the chairman, was the only person he had told that I wanted to talk things over with the full board. It turned out that the board had asked to see me urgently and he had reported back that I did not want to see them. And he had told me quite clearly when I asked to see the board that they wanted nothing to do with me. I suspect that it was a little more than crossed wires but Basil and Harry were powerful figures at Saints and nobody ever challenged him about it.

But while they called the shots behind the scenes it was the Greenalls, Karaliuses and Frank Fosters who settled matters out on the pitch. And if a few noses were broken, teeth loosened or blood spilt along the way, it was all part of the game.

*

No matter what the threats from people such as Harry Cook and Basil Lowe were like, they were nothing compared with the punishment that I could have been made to suffer if I didn't buck up my ideas – at rugby union. Even with all their clout, Cook and Lowe couldn't send me out to some godforsaken place in the Indian Ocean to carry out the rest of my National Service. One man who warned me that that was exactly what would happen if I didn't 'pull my finger out' was my RAF commanding officer.

I was already a rugby league international and a Saints regular at the start of the 1960s when I had to do what every man had to do in those days – two years' National Service. The services were the only place where a professional rugby league player was not treated like some untouchable by the rugby union fraternity. We were even allowed to play the game! Everywhere else, the league man was the great unwashed as far as rugby union was concerned. Today, of course, things are a lot different and players regularly swap codes in an age when both games are fully professional. One code has even been known to pay the other a transfer fee, as in the case of Inga Tuigamala's move from Wigan to Newcastle Falcons. In the 1960s, however, even playing amateur rugby league was taboo for a rugby union player.

But for me and a few others, things were different and I was able to get leave to play for Saints in Saturday games as long as I turned out for the RAF's rugby union team in midweek.

I had only been drafted into the RAF as a result of some wheels-within-wheels dealings. I passed my medical and was expected to be posted to Catterick with the army. However, a knock on my digs door at one o'clock in the morning changed all that. The RAF recruiting officer had called to ask if I had taken my medical and when I told him I had and that I was in the army, the wheels started turning, my papers were retrieved and I was eventually 'transferred' to the RAF for training at Bridgnorth and later to serve at Haydock. Catterick had been fine by me, but Haydock . . . I must have been the only aircraftsman in the forces who had enough time to go home for lunch! Still, it was nice to feel wanted among all the professionals such as doctors and solicitors, so being a professional rugby player came in handy.

I had only been in the service for three days when I was allowed leave to play in the Lancashire Cup final and, providing Saints matches did not clash with Inter-Services rugby union fixtures, I never had a problem. That is, until that threat from Group Captain Cameron that I would be seeing out my RAF days in the Indian Ocean – thousands of miles from Knowsley Road – if I didn't shape up.

The occasion was an RAF match at Cambridge and I was travelling down with two Saints directors to whom I had suggested the club should take a look at a player called Kenneth Williams with a view to signing. Unfortunately, the trip from St Helens to Cambridge was not as smooth as it should have been. The directors decided there was plenty of time and that a meal would break up the journey nicely. Unfortunately, by the time we arrived at Cambridge, the RAF, which had started with only fourteen men, were already trailing and heading for a heavy defeat.

'Get yourself out there, Murphy, and do your stuff – otherwise there'll be no home leave for you . . . the Indian Ocean is a long way from St Helens,' I was told.

I have never concentrated on a game so much in all my life – so much so that I had no time to think that my opposing stand-off (I would never dream of playing scrum-half in rugby union) was England's Richard Sharp.

Not that I was worried about reputations. The thought of spending my days in the middle of nowhere was incentive enough for me to 'pull my finger out'. I managed to have the game of my life, scoring a couple of tries as we won the match comfortably. My home-base posting was safe.

Come to think of it, that's something else Harry Cook

should have been grateful for – he was one of the directors who had landed me with that ultimatum in the first place. If he hadn't decided to stop for a meal I wouldn't have had the worry of winning-at-all-costs in what was only a friendly.

I enjoyed my stint with rugby union, mixed with some great people – officers and men all in it together – as we played many of the top sides from Wales such as Neath, Llanelli and Cardiff, but especially Swansea.

In the RAF team was an officer called Leighton Jenkins, a great fellow but a bit of a leg-puller. An RAF officer he may have been but I am sure some of the Murphy professionalism must have rubbed off on him the day we played Swansea. I played rugby union the same way I played league – treating it professionally – looking for players to support me on a break. In those days, and perhaps the same applies today, it was the wing-forward's job to take care of the half-back. Swansea were blessed with some fine talent and one of their wing-forwards had been called into the Welsh team for his first cap. Naturally enough, he had never heard of me and I had never heard of him, so we started even. I learned later that, before the match, he asked Leighton Jenkins about me and was told: 'You don't have to worry. He's nothing special, just some rugby league lad, but he has got no pace. You can give him the outside without any problems.'

Give me the outside – I couldn't have asked for more. Four times he let me free and when I touched down for the fourth try I could almost hear him cursing to Leighton Jenkins: 'You realise you have just cost me my Welsh cap.'

Although I enjoyed playing rugby union and had some of the best days of my life in the RAF (I was among the last batch to be called up), giving me some moments I will always treasure, there was nothing like the buzz of rugby league for me.

It was good to know that I was well thought of even when we lost. That happened in my Twickenham appearance against the Royal Navy. We were beaten 9–3 but one reporter took the view that I had 'singlehandedly kept the RAF in the game'.

Back at the start of the 1960s it was a great privilege to play at Twickenham, to be considered the equal of or better than some of the players who had appeared there. But if you were to ask me . . . Twickenham or Wembley? Swansea or St Helens? Cardiff or Castleford? It was great to have had the experience, but rugby league was in my blood and, once my RAF days were over, I had to step back across the great divide. I was no longer a serving amateur . . . I was one of the great unwanted in all the best circles. I was back in rugby league and proud of it.

SIX

Hi, Leigh . . . Hi, Leigh . . . Hello

The approach from Leigh came completely out of the blue and, although I have said I would have crawled all the way back to Knowsley Road to play for the Saints, it looked as though even that wasn't going to be good enough for some people.

By then I was feeling bitter towards the club and there was no way back. Even so, a move to Leigh wasn't exactly my idea of a good career move. In any case I was still under contract to St Helens, even though I wasn't being included in their plans.

But Tommy Sale, the Leigh delegate who approached me, had a solution when I told him that I wouldn't be able to take up the offer. 'Don't worry,' he told me, 'we want you as coach. And Saints won't even get a penny.'

Being out of the game for nearly twelve months had almost killed me off, but as there had been no making-up or shaking of hands, that made me chuckle. But I had to admit: 'I haven't coached anybody in my life.'

I was told not to worry about that – Leigh wanted me and were prepared to make me an offer. Alice could hardly believe it – 'You're not going to Leigh!' was her reaction. But I did join the club, and never regretted the decision for a moment. The ties with St Helens had been well and truly cut. But there was something missing. I wasn't playing the game and I was still only twenty-seven.

So I got in touch with one of my press pals and asked him to fly the story that I was thinking about making a return to the game. Suddenly the knives were out. Saints wanted a fee . . . Leigh offered them two thousand pounds . . . and the bargaining began.

Harry Cook said that offer was an insult but with my colours now firmly nailed to the Leigh mast I argued that it was a hell of a lot more than the eighty quid it cost them to sign me. It was not a friendly negotiation.

The Saints chairman reminded me of the bumper testimonial I had received after ten years at the club. Actually it was a 'bumper' two thousand pounds – of which half was already written into my contract anyway!

Harry Cook, who passed away at the age of ninety-five at the end of February 2000, was a St Helens legend, the club's longest-serving chairman, who had spent twenty-five years at the helm. Naturally, he had a great influence on my rugby life and was the man behind the signings of so many local youngsters. He was respected throughout the game and we always addressed him as Mr Cook – never Harry. Despite the final disagreement at the time I left Saints, I loved the man dearly.

As I have already explained, Cook was a powerful force inside the club and he had that great skill that everybody talks about these days: the art of man-management. I know this from personal experience. I remember several occasions when a disgruntled player, looking for a pay rise, would get all steamed up, ready to storm into the office and demand an extra few pounds. Players like Don Vines, Vince Karalius, Dick Huddard – hard men, all of them – will testify to Harry Cook's management skills. They would go into the office ready to stand their ground and come out all smiles after a lengthy meeting.

The first question we would all ask them was: 'Well, how much?'

The answer was always the same: 'We had a good long chat and we shook hands.'

'Yes, but how much did you get?'

'Oh, I didn't get any money – the chairman explained the financial situation and I got the message . . .'

Harry Cook was that sort of man. He was so good at man-management that it was amazing that he didn't get *us* to pay the club for allowing us to play, rather than the other way round.

He was an institution at Knowsley Road, though I don't suppose I saw him quite that way when the time came for me to leave my home-town club.

I knew there was no going back to Saints and in the end I believe the clubs settled on a fee in the region of five thousand pounds. One lesson I did take into my job as player-coach of Leigh was that if a dispute between the club and a player isn't settled within the first two or three weeks then common sense goes out of the window and the row will rumble on until there is only one solution – a parting of the ways. The bitterness and name-calling get worse and you can never discuss reasons or solutions with any logic.

But, in the end, it all worked out. I got to meet some of the nicest people in the game at a small-town club whose supporters, players and directors – everybody from the chairman to the tea lady – appreciated what I was trying to do . . . and what I eventually achieved. It is little wonder that I went back to homely Hilton Park three times over the years and I wouldn't have changed a day of the whole experience.

*

The chairman Jack Ruben and I got off to the best of starts. His opening offer was like music to my ears: 'It's your job to get things right on the field – and money's no problem,' he told me.

I never thought I would ever hear that from any club chairman. I had been around long enough to know that sort of commitment didn't happen everywhere.

But Jack Ruben was different. After all, he had once been the owner of Red Rum who went on to win three Grand Nationals, so I had a great feeling about the place. And when he promised me he would back me in the transfer market, that was good enough for me.

Years later when former Scotland rugby union and Great Britain Test player George Fairbairn took over at Hull Kingston Rovers he was asked by a journalist how things were going in his new job. 'I'll say this for the directors,' George said to the reporter. 'They are men of their word.'

'How come?'

'When I came here they said to me that there was no money available for new players – and they have stuck to that promise.'

But that was not how it was at Leigh – the chairman had promised me cash to spend and as I knew that I could spot a player as well as anybody and better than most, I went shopping. I didn't just rush out and spend all the chairman's money in one shop, however. I let things settle down before I realised that if we were to make any progress we were going to have to add some experience, so I went for trusted men like Laurie Gilfedder, Harry Major and Peter Smethurst. I had spent the grand total of less than two thousand pounds on Gilfedder and Major and was still negotiating with Swinton over Smethurst. Before I could complete the signing, though, I was called into the boardroom to be faced by an irate chairman who demanded to know what I was doing spending all of his money.

I could hardly believe it – I had spent two thousand pounds and was on the carpet for it!

'Look, Mr Ruben,' I said, 'if this is your idea of money being no problem you can stick your job up your –'

But it wasn't . . . he calmed me down and I went on to spend the best two grand any manager ever spent. I defy any other club to come up with a bargain to match the signing of the late Peter Smethurst. Smethurst was a magnificent professional, a winner right down to his toenails. And if anybody doubts that, they should get their hands on a tape of the Leigh v. Leeds 1971 Challenge Cup final and follow Peter Smethurst around the Wembley pitch.

The day he signed I knew what I was getting. The chairman was explaining what the terms were: winning money is such and such; losing money is . . . And before he could even finish the sentence, Smethurst interrupted: 'I'm not interested in the losers' pay. I want to play for him and I want to win summat!'

And he did – a coveted Challenge Cup winners' medal with little Leigh.

*

If the signing of Peter Smethurst gave me the most satisfaction, there were a few others not far behind. Dave Chisnall, Jimmy Fiddler, Jeff Clarkson – who must have played for every club in the game and a few more besides – were up there with the best. But one signing I made saved me from a bloody good hiding.

I was still on the look-out to improve the team when we came up against Rochdale Hornets who, like ourselves, were a small-town team trying to make it big among the glamour boys of the game. It is no secret that there are two positions on a rugby league field that are filled by players whose qualities include an outrageous cheek and a mean streak with an enthusiasm for turning nasty if the chance ever came.

Leigh v. Rochdale Hornets had two such players – Alex Murphy (Leigh) and Kevin Ashcroft, the Rochdale hooker who actually came from Leigh. We had been going at it hammer and tongs all afternoon and the referee, apart from giving the occasional penalty to cool things down, had let us get on with it.

It was after one particular blow-up that brought us another lecture that I turned on Ashcroft and snapped: 'This isn't over yet. After the match, you and me, behind the stand – we'll finish it there.'

I expected him to laugh it off and walk away. No such luck. Instead he looked me straight in the eye and said, 'You're on, Murphy.'

Now, I didn't scare easily but the idea of going behind the stand and slugging it out with Kevin Ashcroft was not my idea of the ideal way to finish a game. We got through the match and Ashcroft had a blinder. But it wasn't over. I fully expected Ash to be waiting for me so I said to the chairman: 'We need a hooker and Ashcroft is the man I want to boost this team.' I didn't tell him that I was trying to avoid a bloody nose but he judged me on my other signings and gave the go-ahead.

As it turned out, Ashcroft and I became close friends – he followed me to Warrington and Salford as assistant coach. I still wonder what would have happened if we had decided to settle our differences behind the stand instead of combining our efforts to turn Leigh and then Warrington into the teams of the 1970s.

Another of my successful signings was Dave Chisnall. The way the game is played nowadays, Chizzy would probably be written off as one of those roly-poly forwards who ate all the pies – a dinosaur from a bygone age when, today's fans would have you believe, every prop-forward had a beer belly and couldn't run a hundred yards in less than half a minute. Well, despite his shape – and even he would find it hard to argue with the suggestion that he wasn't exactly built for a career in modelling – Chisnall was a superb forward, quick on his feet with a great sidestep . . . and a fuse to match. He wouldn't have been the player he was if he hadn't got involved and, although he often got on the wrong side of opponents and referees, he was a great asset to me.

Chisnall was not every referee's favourite player – and he had his own ideas about them. Top of his hate list was Leigh whistler Stan Wall. Chisnall loathed him with a passion – he was always getting into trouble with Stan so when the chance came to get his own back he made the most of it.

Being a local, Stan asked me if he could join the Leigh players on their training sessions. In those days players and officials used to mix and mingle so the request was nothing out of the ordinary. It was only when Dave Chizzy heard about it that I started to have reservations.

'Stan Wall? I hate him!' Chisnall reminded me.

'Just stay away from him – don't say anything, just get on with your own training.'

Some hopes. Like every club, we finished our training sessions with a game of touch-and-pass – where the only bodily contact was a simple tap on the shoulder to indicate a tackle. To keep Stan involved – you never knew when you might need a favour in the future – I let him join in, sticking him out on the wing out of harm's way. By the end of the session I had forgotten all about Chisnall's deep-rooted dislike of one of our top referees. And Stan himself clearly had no idea. It was only when one of the players did what comes naturally and threw the ball out wide and Stan Wall was there waiting did I get an inkling of what was about to happen. Too late.

Stan, who is now on the training staff at St Helens, was never what you would call a big fella – ten stone dripping wet would be my guess. And, as I have already suggested, Dave was no gazelle. But it was only touch-and-pass – nothing could happen. It was a good thing I didn't bet on it. Chisnall's idea of a 'touch' when the two collided was to send our guest spinning towards the grandstand. All the years of hate brought about by long lectures, finger-wagging and instant dismissals went into that one shoulder-charge. I thought he had killed the poor bloke.

Happily, Stan eventually came back to the land of the living while Chisnall was safe in the knowledge that there was nothing his poor victim could do about it. As long as Chisnall played for Leigh, he would never come across Stan Wall in a serious rugby match. There was a rule that prevented referees taking charge of games involving their home-town club. Chizzy's best hope was that Stan wasn't thinking of moving house!

But, for all his size and strength, Dave Chisnall did not always come out on top in his run-ins with an old 'un. In later years, when we had linked up again at Warrington and Dave was a little older but not a lot wiser, we had a co-ordinator called Tommy Lomax. A former boxer, Tommy was by then pushing seventy if he was a day. He was saddled with the unfortunate nickname of 'Lino' Lomax – because rumour had it that he spent most of his boxing career on the floor.

Chizzy would be the first to admit that he was not the most co-ordinated of players – indeed he hardly saw the point of what Tommy was trying to teach. 'Why are we doing this, Lino?' 'What's the point of that, Lino?' 'A waste of bloody time if you ask me, Lino.'

As you can imagine, Tommy hated being called Lino. Dave knew it – we all knew it – but he never stopped, at least not until the day when Tommy decided enough was enough. They were yelling at each other with Tommy demanding satisfaction – a bit like the old West – in the only way he knew how: in the boxing ring. Now, a long-retired boxer with a reputation for spending most of his career on his back and a powerful young rugby league forward is a mismatch that even Don King would not try to foist on a gullible American public. And so it turned out – one punch and Tommy had ended once and for all any further reference to Lino Lomax. Dave's pride was hurt as much as his chin but I am sure he saw my assistant in a different light from that day onwards.

*

Although the time at Leigh gave me some of the best years of my life, all good things must come to an end. But when I eventually left Hilton Park – for the first time – it was under a bit of a cloud. And, like so many times in the past, I got the blame for something that was not my fault.

I had built up a good team at Leigh. Being player-coach of a successful club gets you noticed and the rumours about my future started well before we made it to Wembley and that victory over Leeds. I had had talks with Warrington and I must have impressed them because they offered me a job. But I still had unfinished business at Hilton Park and all I could promise Warrington was that I would give them an answer once Leigh were knocked out of the Challenge Cup. Clearly the Warrington directors did not expect us to go all the way so they said that would be fine and the job would be there when I was free to join them.

I told the new Leigh chairman, Jack Harding, about the offer and my promise to stick with Leigh as long as we were in the Cup. He seemed happy enough with that and we went about business as usual.

Things just got better and better that season, and after scraping a boring win over Huddersfied in the semis we were on our way to the now dearly departed Twin Towers. I couldn't understand why the bookies had made Leeds the 5–1 on favourites to win the Cup because, although we were unfashionable and they were the glamour boys, we were the better team.

And I believe the Cup was on its way to Leigh from the moment the players first set foot inside the stadium on the day before the final. We had already arrived, dressed in club suits and blazers, had done the royal-box thing – climbing the steps for a mock Cup presentation. It was a scorching-hot day and the players were in awe of the place.

We had just about wrapped things up when the Leeds

team arrived for their pre-Wembley walkabout. They sauntered around in denim jackets, jeans, tracksuit bottoms – a real rag-bag outfit who got right up everybody's nose. 'Look at that lot,' I said. 'Arrogant bastards – they think all they have to do tomorrow is turn up and collect the Cup.'

From that moment Leigh couldn't wait to get at them. Our confidence was sky high and it was boosted even further when we picked six winners on the visit to the dog track. We could do no wrong.

And the carry-over to the Saturday is now part of rugby league folklore. The dismissal of Syd Hines, the day of the underdog, for me the Lance Todd Trophy and all was well with the world. At least for twenty-four hours.

The Wembley triumph under our belts, we returned home to the expected rousing reception – though not everybody in the town was thrilled to bits about the win. Bert Hulme, a member of the club board, was also a local bookmaker and did he catch a cold! At the start of the Cup run he had offered odds of 66–1 against us lifting the trophy. Being a bit of a betting man myself, I had a slice of that – and advised the players to do the same. 'It's like stealing sweets from kids,' I told them.

All I could say to our boardroom bookie was that his money was all going to a worthy cause. But, even in our moment of triumph I knew that my days at the club were numbered. I had reminded Jack Harding that the offer from Warrington was on the table but I felt there was still a future for me at Leigh. However, I told him that if he wanted me to stay he would have to make money available for new players. It was then that I discovered the club's ambitions did not match my own.

'What do you want to buy new players for?' he argued. 'Haven't we just won the Cup?'

The suggestion was that what we had was good enough to take us even higher. I knew it wasn't so I told them I would be going to Warrington. It was then that the whole thing turned sour. Harding accused me of walking out on the club without a word and the fans believed him. Murphy was the villain of the piece again and only I knew the truth.

I didn't know then that I would go back to Leigh a few years later and we would become rugby league champions for the first time in more than seventy-five years. A lot of water was to pass under the bridge before that could happen.

SEVEN

Men behaving badly . . . or, have a drink on us, Mister Chairman

Warrington had fallen on hard times when Ossie Davis came to the rescue. They were deeply in debt and facing the possibility of having to bring in the receivers when Mr Davis and Brian Pitchford rode in like the cavalry.

Ossie Davis announced to the board – a group of well-meaning people who were simply out of their depth – that he would take over all their debts and allow the club to start afresh. This, quite naturally, was greeted with loud applause from everybody in the room. But – and there was always going to be a but – there was one minor condition. They all waited in silence for the announcement.

'I want you all to resign.'

That was the state of the club I joined in my second job as a player-coach having left Leigh in a far better state than when I arrived.

The boardroom coup went through and Messrs Davis and Pitchford, high-powered businessmen in their own right, set about making Warrington into the team of the 1970s. They were the sort of people I believed could match my own ambitions. I would have trusted Ossie Davis with my life, and Brian Pitchford eventually became one of my closest friends.

Davis was director of a huge building company and commanded great respect, but first impressions were not favourable. He invited me for talks about the job of player-coach but before I made my final decision I suggested I should go along to watch the team play. It was not the happiest day of my life. They were playing Huddersfield – and they were so bad the crowd were throwing rotten fruit at them!

The club was in deep financial trouble when Davis and Pitchford put their ultimatum to the board and together with secretary Phil Worthington set about rebuilding the entire structure. So, in May 1971, I embarked on my second job but only after telling Ossie Davis: 'There's a hell of a lot of work to be done.'

'Don't you worry about that – you look after the rugby, I'll look after the finance.'

That was the start of a partnership and a friendship that would see me through the Warrington job for seven years in which we won every trophy going.

My first signing was Ian Potter from Leigh who cost us two thousand pounds – getting in ahead of St Helens who were also keen to sign him. I was surprised when, only weeks after getting to Wembley, the board were prepared to sell many of the players who had done them so well – and to a club who could do them so much damage!

I turned to tried and trusted friends – men whom I had

taken to Leigh such as Kevin Ashcroft, Jeff Clarkson and David Chisnall. These were men I had left behind but would dearly love to have on board for the new Warrington.

And I couldn't have done it without a helping hand from a few of my pals in the press. Over the years I had built up a good relationship with the likes of Jack Bentley of the *Daily Express*, Joe Humphreys from the *Mirror*, Eddie Waring and a few more. So a quick phone call to them usually brought results along the lines of Warrington are interested in Leigh's Wembley hooker Kevin Ashcroft (or David Chisnall or David Eckersley or whoever I was still hoping to sign). These articles would be followed by strong denials from Leigh and words to the effect that 'nobody is leaving this club'. It usually took between two and three weeks for the headline to read: 'Warrington get their man'.

I bought two players from Swinton – Mike and Barry Philbin – and then, still in a rush to put a team together, I placed an advertisement in the national papers. One of the men to answer it was Mike Nicholas, a forward with Aberavon. He had been playing in a seven-a-side tournament in Scotland and called in at Warrington on his way home. The ad had already brought me two players – Denis Curling from Bedford and Welshman Clive Jones.

Nicholas breezed into the place full of confidence. 'I believe you have signed Clive Jones,' he challenged, and when I told him I had, he said: 'Then why don't you sign me? I'm twice as good a player as he is.'

So we did – and he was. And there were many times when I felt that his unscheduled stop-over at Warrington on his way back from the sevens was the best thing that ever happened to the club.

It wasn't always sweetness and light with Mike Nick,

however. I once had to talk my way out of a scrape with him after we had lost by a single point at Whitehaven. I laid the blame firmly on Mike's shoulders because he had hung on to the ball when he had a three-man overlap. I made it known in no uncertain terms that, big as he was, it was his fault. In my frustration, the only way I could think of getting through to him was to challenge him to a fight! When I saw that he was ready and eager to take me up on it, I had to do some fast talking to stay in one piece. Team coach or not, Mike Nick was having none of that.

Probably his finest hour came at Wembley in 1974. I had promised the men who had given me the Warrington job – Ossie Davis and Brian Pitchford – that I would take the club to the top – and to every rugby league fan in the land that meant a trip to Wembley. Warrington had not been there for twenty years – in 1954 they had been involved in the only drawn final at the stadium before winning the Cup in a replay watched by 102,000 fans at Bradford's Odsal Bowl – so there was a bit of catching up to do.

The previous season we had won the League Leaders Trophy, topping the thirty-club division and losing only five of our thirty-eight games. But defeat in the semi-final of the play-offs by eventual champions Dewsbury was a disappointing end to the season.

It was Dewsbury who provided the semi-final opposition in the Challenge Cup and a 17–7 victory at Wigan took us to Wembley just three years after I had joined Warrington. It was hardly one of Wembley's most memorable occasions but for me it was something special. By leading out Warrington I was setting a proud record of captaining three different teams in a Wembley Cup final, following St Helens in 1966 and Leigh in 1971. Warrington won the game against

Featherstone 24–9 with Mike Nicholas scoring the final try of the afternoon.

Warrington were where I had promised to take them – at the top of the tree. Somehow it almost went totally pear-shaped a few days later when the players were all ordered to attend a celebration party in the hallowed rooms of Chester Town Hall. Brian Pitchford and I had become close friends and he was always someone I could turn to for help and advice during what were eight of the best years of my life. And I can therefore only take part of the responsibility for almost landing him with an embarrassing court appearance only a couple of days after the Wembley victory.

I am not sure he and Ossie Davis were using their heads when they accepted an invitation to show off the Challenge Cup to Chester's civic leaders the following week. It was Mr Davis who gave the royal command. 'Now, this is very important to the club, Alex,' he told me. 'The players are all to attend, dressed in dinner suits and on their best behaviour. This is a special occasion and we must be seen to be doing things properly.'

I did my level best to persuade him that it was not a good idea to introduce some of the players to what for them would be High Society. But he would not take no for an answer and I was left to persuade the players that the good name of the club depended on them staying sober and conducting themselves with decorum.

'It's for Mr Pitchford's sake, not mine,' I told them, remembering that he had introduced me to the Savoy Grill and a lifestyle far removed from Thatto Heath.

They promised to behave – and they did. It was almost too perfect: not a word out of place during the speeches, not a glass broken and everybody stone-cold sober. Ossie

Davis approached me with a deep smile of satisfaction on his face. 'Well done, Alex – and, as a thank-you to the lads, I think we will stop at a pub on the way home for a few drinks.'

'I don't think that is such a good idea, Mr Davis,' I said. 'The players have had a nice time, a pleasant evening. I think we should go straight back to the club –'

But he would have none of it: 'Not at all, there's nothing they can do to spoil my evening now. It has been a great success.'

So, we stopped at a pub and had a few drinks. And then a few more drinks. Some three hours later we piled back on the coach and headed for home. The coach had barely left the carpark when Mike Philbin came staggering down the aisle to where Brian Pitchford and Ossie Davis were sitting. Well the worse for wear after the dozen or so pints he must have drunk during the stop-over at the pub, Mike leaned over and asked Mr Pitchford, 'Would you like a drink?'

Ever the gentleman, the man we all knew as The Little General, answered: 'That's very kind of you, Michael. I wouldn't say no to a brandy.'

'One brandy coming up,' he said and with that was back up to the rear of the coach to return seconds later, not with a glass but with a bottle. Mr Davis settled for a beer, duly delivered by the same Michael Philbin, and the party swung back into Warrington with everybody in fine spirits.

It was only the following morning that the events of the previous evening came to light. 'Mr Davis would like to see you in the boardroom' was the message waiting for me when I arrived at the ground. So off I went – and knew immediately there was trouble ahead. Mr Davis had removed his glasses and was slowly and deliberately cleaning the lenses –

a sure sign that he was in a serious mood. The conversation went something along these lines:

Mr Davis: 'Alex, you remember that pub we stopped at last night?'

AJM: 'Yes, Mr Chairman, and very nice it was, too.'

Mr Davis: 'Yes, but a bit expensive, don't you think?'

AJM: 'How come, Mr Chairman? The players all paid for their own drinks, apart from the first round which you bought.'

Mr Davis: 'Then perhaps you can explain why we have been landed with a drinks bill of £1,500?'

A look of total innocence was required. 'I don't think I understand,' I lied. Of course I understood. Using two men as look-outs and one on board the coach, the players had systematically emptied the pub's wine and spirits stock via a pair of double windows at the side of the pub. Brandy, whisky, vodka, champagne and all kinds of wine and beer had been loaded aboard the coach.

'Sort it,' said the chairman, who clearly did not believe me.

Back in the dressing-room I told the players what I'd been ordered to do and there were looks of horror on a number of faces when I suggested that there would be big trouble if the money wasn't repaid.

'But we can't afford to pay that back,' they said, almost in unison. But when I pointed out that their Wembley win bonus would do the job nicely there was a sudden change of heart, an immediate show of remarkable one-for-all team spirit, and the money was found.

I reported back to the chairman that the matter was, as he put it, 'sorted'. I was perhaps pushing my luck when I suggested to Brian Pitchford that he should make a contribution. 'For the brandy,' I reminded him.

He protested that he did not know the drink had been stolen but when I argued that he drank it nevertheless, he knocked the price of a bottle off the players' contribution and coughed up. Warrington was that sort of club – the spirit stretched right from the chairman down to the tea ladies and the cleaners.

A year later we were back at Wembley but this time I was not there as a player and could only watch as local rivals Widnes won 14–7, their only try coming from another of the man-mountains from Wales, Jim Mills. John Bevan scored Warrington's try.

A second John Player Trophy victory – 9–4 against Widnes – brought my silverware collection for Warrington to six trophies (and we reached three other finals) before I moved on to the next challenge. But what a vastly different chapter in the Life and Times of Alex Murphy that turned out to be. The move to Salford was not the best I ever made.

EIGHT

Murph the Mouth and other names

It was the *Daily Mirror* that landed me with the name and, although it seemed a good idea at the time, it was something I became lumbered with after my retirement from the game . . . and even before that. Murph the Mouth – that was the banner heading above my weekly column in the *Mirror* and, being the sort of outspoken person I am I tried to live up to the paper's expectations. If I trod on a few toes now and again, so much the better.

I may have mellowed a bit since those days but anybody who thinks I am ready to take things back or that I didn't really mean it, are wrong. I meant every word. The fact that the *Mirror* put into headlines what a lot of people had thought about me for a long time only encouraged me not to let anybody down – my supporters and critics alike knew exactly where they stood.

The chance to go into print with my views and opinions did not come until I had reached the end of my career, of course, although rugby league journalists knew long before then that they could rely on me to tell it like it was. If they ever needed a quote to back up a piece they would turn to me. They might not have liked what I said, but I always made myself available.

I made a lot of friends in the rugby league press and that friendship was built on trust. You read in today's sports pages how the high-profile heroes of the 1990s are being hounded by the press wherever they go; that the sight of a reporter's notepad or tape-recorder sends them into a panic. It was never like that in the days when a rugby league player, however famous, however many Test caps he had to his name or cup winners' medals or championship titles he had won, was part of the community. There was always somebody living in the same street or going to the same job who would be ready to bring you down a peg or two if you got too big for your boots.

I might have mentioned somewhere that I had the reputation of being a cocky little bugger. Well, my peg-or-two of a comedown arrived before I had even set out on my international career. And it happened twice. The reason might be simple enough – that I was a slow learner. I'll leave you to judge for yourself.

Without wishing to wallow in nostalgia – dammit, why not? – I think it is fair to say that the 1958 Battle of Brisbane was British rugby league's finest hour, and the 1962 tour party was the best squad of players ever to leave these shores. Some people might want to argue with the second view but there is no doubt whatsoever about the first. All I can say is that I am proud to have been there both times, even though

I was already building up a bit of a reputation as Murph the Mouth. It almost cost me my place on the first trip.

Strange though it may seem coming from someone as sure about his abilities as I was, I was surprised and thrilled to be chosen for a tour trial in 1958. I had established myself in the St Helens team at the age of eighteen and my form at the time was good. Even so, there would only be two half-backs going in the party and as far as I could see the decision on who should fill those places was already cut and dried – Jeff Stevenson of Leeds and Oldham's Frank Pitchford were the best of the bunch . . . and an impressive bunch it was, too. So I was delighted to be included even though I felt I was only there to shake things up a bit. Mind you, that did not stop me from talking myself up – only I picked on the wrong man to make my point.

Rugby league in those days was run by one man (no, not Maurice Lindsay!) – Bill Fallowfield. *Mister* Fallowfield to any player who valued his career. The headmasterish overlord of the game that was run from Chapeltown Road in Leeds was the Godfather of the Game and that meant he was in charge from top to bottom – from the international down to the humble pub amateur. Mr Fallowfield, an ex-rugby union player with Northampton, was not known for his sense of humour, and I suppose I should have known better than to make the remark that almost cost me a whole Test career. I knew I had had a good game in the trial so, as soon as it was over, I went across to Bill Fallowfield, the man who would have the final say on which twenty-six players went to Australia for the Ashes series.

'Well, who are the other twenty-five who are going with me?' I asked him.

If looks could have killed I would have shrivelled up and

died on the spot. It was obvious I had picked the wrong man. He slapped me down so badly I thought I had blown any chance of making the flight.

'*If* you get picked,' he said, 'and it's a big *if*, the first thing I'd do is take a pin and put so many punctures in that big head of yours, you'd end up . . .' He walked away in exasperation and I was left standing there wondering.

I told Alan Prescott, a teammate at St Helens and the man who was going to be tour captain, what had happened and that I thought I had blown my chances. Of course, I still believed that Stevenson and Pitchford were the men who would be going on the tour and not me. I found out later that Prescott had had a word with Fallowfield and the big boss had calmed down enough to include me in the squad. But what was joy for me was obviously disappointment for somebody else – and it turned out that Frank Pitchford was the one to miss out.

Great though it was to be going on tour, I thought that, as I was still only eighteen, I would be going along just for the experience. I had never played international rugby so it was obvious that I would be number two to Stevenson. I felt sorry for Pitchford, but as luck would have it he got on the trip anyway when Jeff Stevenson had to pull out. Even then I thought I would be going as the understudy, only this time to Pitchford instead of Stevenson.

As things turned out I could not have been further from the mark – but for a second time I allowed my big mouth to run away with me and I almost became the archetype for that old Brian Clough story about the footballer who got two international caps in one day – his first and his last!

I was not even dreaming of making the Test team and although in my own mind I believed I was playing well enough, I genuinely thought that the number 7 jersey at Sydney Cricket Ground would be worn by Frank Pitchford of Oldham.

Once again, I had Alan Prescott to thank. I am convinced the tour managers were not ready to take a chance on an upstart of a young kid with no international experience for a Test that would attract a hostile capacity crowd to one of the world's most famous grounds. 'Precky' thought differently. He thought I was up to it and, when the team was announced, there was my name in the scrum-half spot, ready to make my international début.

I was like the cat that had got the cream . . . and it showed. It was a few days before the first Test that I came across the man who was to be my opposing scrum-half. We were at a local racetrack when Prescott introduced a few of us to three guys I had never seen before. As we went through the formalities and I was shaking hands with this chunky hard-nosed Aussie, Prescott said something along the lines of: 'I'd like you to meet the best scrum-half in the world.' I jumped in with my usual cocky quip: 'It's nice of you to say so – even before I have played a single Test match.'

Not for the first time I got that look – the one that could kill. The man I was being introduced to was none other than the great Australian scrum-half Keith Holman. Without saying a word he gave me the look. And it said: I'll wipe that silly smile off your face come Saturday.

Saturday came and there was a packed Sydney Cricket Ground and I was soon to wish that Holman had stuck to dirty looks to bring me down a peg or two! I decided that, although he looked like a square brick outhouse, I wasn't going to let him boss me about. Just to show him that I wasn't to be messed with, I decided that the first chance I got I would run straight at him and show him who was in charge of this Test match. It was not the brightest idea I had ever had and it was amazing I still had any brains left to think with after he had finished with me. At the first tackle he picked me up and for one awful moment I thought he was going to throw me into the stand!

The next tackle was even worse – a piledriver into the turf that had he done it any harder, would have seen me come out somewhere near Dewsbury. But did I learn? Did I hell!

He got to me, and the longer the game went on, the worse it got. I had a nightmare. It was my first Test match and it looked as though it was going to be my last. We were beaten 25–8 and it was all my fault. At least, that's the way I was seeing things when I got back to my hotel room. I was close to tears, feeling really sorry for myself and thinking my career was over.

It was then that I learned just how much I owed to Alan Prescott, the tour captain. He came into the room and although he was the most mild-mannered of rugby players, he gave me a rocket, a dressing-down that shook me rigid. I was staring down at the floor, still brooding like a spoilt kid when he tore into me, calling me a total idiot. I couldn't face him.

'Look at me when I am talking to you,' he demanded, 'and stop feeling sorry for yourself. If you ever want to play rugby league for Great Britain again you're going to have to get something into your head. What is your biggest asset, Spud?' he said, trying the quiet, fatherly approach.

I shrugged. 'Speed, I suppose.'

'Exactly – so why did you spend all afternoon squaring up to Keith Holman? Next time, I want to see you running away from him – and if you ever let him tackle you again you'll feel my boot up your backside.'

And then, just to remind me that his talking-to did not mean I was out of the woods, he added: 'That's if there is a next time.'

There was – thanks to Alan Prescott – and it was, for me, the greatest performance by any national sports team anywhere in the world. Ever. And I don't exaggerate. There was a three-week gap between the first and second Tests and in that time Alan Prescott persuaded the tour manager Tom Mitchell that I was the man for the job in Brisbane.

Tom was going to pick Frank Pitchford, and I, for one, would not have blamed him. But Precky stepped in and spoke up for me. Tom told me later that he took some convincing. After all, I had been a catastrophe in Sydney and Pitchford was the obvious choice. The tour captain told Tom that I had learned my lesson and I promised I would never let him or the team down again.

'Not many people had tried to run through Keith Holman and lived to tell the story,' Prescott told Tom Mitchell. 'And, besides, you would wreck the kid's confidence for good.'

It's doubtful that Tom Mitchell believed that line but he picked me anyway and I was part of that greatest-ever victory. The Battle of Brisbane was more than just another Test match – it was the story of a team who, with all the odds stacked against them, a team of walking wounded who had been written off as no-hopers, a team led by a man with a broken arm dangling uselessly by his side, defied all logic to silence the baying Australians screaming for more Pommie blood. And not only silence them but beat them.

Brisbane, Australia, 5 July 1958, is a day that will live for ever in rugby league folklore. It was a day that belonged to Alan Prescott. In those days there were no substitutes allowed . . . no forwards running off and on the field every ten minutes for a rest or a bucketful of water. If you went off that was it – your team had to manage without you.

Great Britain were already one down in the series so a second defeat would have meant that the Ashes – the very prize we had come to collect – would stay in Australia. The story of the Battle of Brisbane has been told many times but believe me whatever you have read or heard about the game doesn't get close to what it was really like out there with thirty-two thousand partisan fans screaming for blood, a dressing-room that looked like the accident and emergency department of a major hospital, and only nine fit players to face a team of Australians already riding high after their first victory.

It was always going to be a bruising, bitter struggle with a few old scores to be settled from Sydney but nobody had figured on what damage could be done in the course of one rugby match. David Bolton, our stand-off, suffered a damaged collarbone and was out of the match; Jim Challinor, our centre, copped a badly damaged elbow, and Eric Fraser suffered the same injury and we were down to only nine fit men.

But the worst of all was still to come. Out on the field that day was a man who should have had a medal cut in his honour for bravery. Schoolboy stories of Captain Marvel and Captain Fantastic don't even come close to describing the courage of Britain's rugby league captain that day, when Alan Prescott played for most of the match with a broken arm.

It was in the dressing-room at half-time that I really learned what playing for your country is all about and I knew when Prescott led us out for the second half we were going to win. Vince Karalius, one of the men the Aussies always feared, moved from his customary role in the pack to partner me at stand-off in place of David Bolton. We were in an attacking position when he suddenly turned to me and said: 'Okay, Spud, let's put on a move.'

I rasped back: 'Bloody hell, Vinty, we haven't got enough people on the field to try any fancy stuff.'

As it turned out, we tried a runaround that caught the Australians napping and I went in to score.

Shortly afterwards, he said: 'Time to try another?'

'Let's forget it – quit while we're ahead,' I told him, and this time he got the message.

As it happened, we had no choice but to play open, expansive rugby – there weren't enough of us to crowd them out. And through it all, Alan Prescott led from the front. Although his arm was dangling uselessly at his side, he didn't flinch and in the end Britain won the second Test 25–18. It was the match that saved the Tour and had the Australian fans, who had started the day by booing the poor Poms, cheering us off. They didn't like losing but they knew they had seen a magnificent achievement. Their crowd, their ground, their greats, even their ref – we had seen them off and with only nine fit players and the heart of Alan Prescott. I am a believer in miracles – and that was some sort of miracle. Keith Holman? Sorry, I forgot – I never even noticed he was playing.

The effects of the Brisbane battle were staggering. A fortnight later nearly seventy thousand spectators jammed into Sydney Cricket Ground to see the Poms get their comeuppance. They left disappointed. We massacred them 40–17 to win the rugby league Ashes in Australia for the first time in a dozen years. And to think I almost talked my way out of it all . . .

It was the 1958 tour that was the forerunner to the smash-hit stage show *No Sex Please, We're British*. At least that is how it seems now. There we were, twenty-six healthy and fit young lads with healthy and fit appetites who were shunted off to a training camp at Surfers Paradise a week before a Test match. Now Surfers is not exactly the place to look if you're searching for a nunnery or a monastery. It is the St Tropez, *Baywatch*-type place where the bikinis are smaller than handkerchiefs and the girls almost wearing them are definitely not the shy, retiring types. You would hardly expect rugby training and tackle shields to be able to attract the sort of attention necessary in the face of some fierce competition. Strangely, there was never a hint of a player abandoning his duty or forgetting the cause of winning a Test series. It would be nice to look back and think what a dedicated squad of devoted young athletes we all were. It would, I suspect, be much more accurate to record that the British management team of Barney Manson, Jim Brough and Tom Mitchell knew exactly what they were doing when they doctored the tea with bromide! Surfers Paradise could have been St Helens Rec for all the effect the place had on any of us. Sex was definitely off the menu.

And if sex was a no-no, so was the five-star treatment that is given to today's rugby league player abroad. Not for us the Sheraton Wentworth or the Manly Pacific with its indoor pool and rooftop jacuzzi, televisions and *à la carte* restaurants. For the Brits abroad in 1958, the last word in luxury was a ramshackle old pub in Sydney called the Olympic which had one way in and one way out and, on the management's instructions, an eleven o'clock curfew that, almost always, was obeyed.

Vince Karalius, later to be dubbed the Wild Bull of the Pampas by Aussies smart enough to know that you didn't mess with Vinty, was one tourist who did manage to break the curfew and get away with it. Vinty arrived back after a night out to find that the door was locked. Or so he thought. After one gentle push and a curse he was left with the prospect of scrambling over a row of sheds at the back, up a drainpipe and knocking on a window to be let in. Looking like somebody who had been dragged though a hedge backwards instead of having made a quiet visit to the cinema, Vince was eventually hauled aboard, satisfied that he had not been spotted by the management. It was while he was still congratulating himself on his excellent piece of deception that Alan Davies pushed open the door and strode boldly into the hotel. It appeared that Vince had given the wrong side of the double doors a shove and not tried the other.

'That's why you're in the forwards and not among the glamour boys in the backs. Brawn is no substitute for brains, Vinty,' said St Helens teammate Glyn Moses.

*

If the 1958 series was all about courage under fire and backs-to-the-wall heroics, the next trip in 1962 was the one that, even today, is regarded as having the strongest party ever to tour abroad. In 1958 the Australian supporters had come to respect us, appreciate our talents and had – eventually – acknowledged that the likes of Dick Huddart, Brian McTigue, Eric Ashton, Alan Davies, Phil Jackson, Prescott, Karalius and Brian Edgar were the world stars of the game. We had put British rugby league up there on the map. So, four years later and with some of those names still around, the Aussies had a good idea what to expect from the Poms. And we didn't disappoint them. Today's full-time players, whether internationals or simply solid club footballers, lay claim to superior fitness, strength and speed over the players of the old days. It is always difficult to compare generations, but to discount Huddart, Karalius, Davies, Ashton and the rest as less fit is an insult to superb footballers.

Today's player may very well be better equipped as a weight-lifter or an arm-wrestler – but as a rugby league player? I don't think so. For instance, those part-timers had played up to sixty matches with their clubs during the winter season before going out on tour to play up to thirty more – including some of the fiercest Test matches ever played – in various parts of Australia. Brian Edgar, one of the most underrated forwards ever to have played the game of rugby league, was a big man with a sidestep; Dick Huddart from Whitehaven and then St Helens was as fast as any of today's forwards and would be a sensation if he was playing nowadays: the 1962 Tour party was full of such great names.

Mick Sullivan was a better winger than anybody ever gave him credit for and Ike Southwood could not even get into the starting line-up. But there was more to Mick Sullivan than just his football ability. He even managed to get the Australians to pick a Test player that suited him!

The man in question was Olympic-rated sprinter Mick Cleary who was later to become a high-ranking member of the Australian government. Sully spread the news all around Sydney that Cleary was by far and away the best winger in the country. Sully made such a point of it that the Australian selectors took his views to heart and promptly picked Cleary on the wing.

Sully was delighted – he had got Cleary into the team so that he could play against him. Mind you, his choice of opposition didn't do me any favours – I ended up with a broken arm tackling the Australian and didn't play on the New Zealand leg of the tour where we lost two Tests in Auckland. But we had done what we set out to do – win the Ashes.

I believe that was the series that turned out to be a watershed for the game in both continents. Historians of the game will point to the 1982 Invincibles as the team who shook rugby league to its foundations. True enough, players like Peter Sterling, Mal Meninga, Brett Kenny, Wally Lewis, Wayne Pearce and the rest of the squad who made up that undefeated Kangaroo party were true greats of the game. But I believe the biggest shake-up happened some twenty years earlier and the game, as an international contest, has never recovered.

In 1962 Eric Ashton had made even Reg Gasnier look ordinary. A year later the whole game was turned on its head. The Australians were still smarting from that series defeat in 1962 – they had won the third Test in Sydney by a single point but the Aussies weren't the sort of people to kid themselves that winning the third game when the series was already lost meant a great deal, especially when it was the result of some of the most one-sided, one-eyed refereeing that it had ever been my misfortune to come across.

So they did something about it. They started to produce a succession of incredible players. Gasnier was to become one of the world's finest centres; Johnny Raper, Graham Langlands and Peter Dimond were all world class; and the 1963 tourists took the Ashes home from these shores for the first time since 1912. They thrashed us at Wembley, winning 28–2, and that man Gasnier got a hat-trick. The biggest humiliation was still to come. It happened in front of thirty-one thousand spectators at Swinton's long-gone Station

Road ground. The Australians created a Test record with a 50–12 victory in a game in which Britain were down to eleven men because of injuries. But neither that nor the fact that we won a brawl of a third Test at Leeds could disguise the fact that Australia's star was in the ascendancy and Britain's was on the wane.

If anybody needs reminding of it, the fact is that, at the start of the twenty-first century we have not won a home series against the old enemy since 1959. And we have not won a series Down Under since 1970. To me that suggests that our 1962 Tourists taught the Australians a lesson they took to heart. The Aussies love winners and they were not winning enough in the world of rugby league. They put it right by the time they came to tour Britain in 1963.

I am sorry to say I never got another crack at them after that. The worst thing is I have nobody to blame but myself. By the time of the next tour – 1966 – I was twenty-six years old and in my prime. My form was good and I was sure to get a place in the squad and but I wanted more than that. I wanted to be captain. I had been on two tours, I had the experience, and in my eyes I was perfect for the job. But the selectors obviously didn't think so – they made Leeds loose-forward Harry Poole the tour captain ahead of me. It was a massive blow to my pride and, in a fit of pique, I acted like a spoilt kid and told them what they could do with their tour. I spat the dummy out of the pram and I'm not proud of it.

Looking back in later years I felt as though I had deserted my country – that I was some kind of traitor. Wilf Spavin, the tour manager, tried to talk me round, but I had made up my mind. I told him I had business commitments that I couldn't leave behind. It was pitiful, really: I had a little joinery business that could have waited.

He was persuasive, telling me that it was more than likely I would be captain anyway because there was every chance that Harry Poole wouldn't even make the Test team. But that wasn't good enough for me – tour captain or nothing was my ultimatum. So it ended up as nothing and, as it turned out, the selectors were right. Harry Poole did not make it into the Test team. We lost the series 2–1 and that was effectively the end of the line for me as a Great Britain player.

I did make one more appearance five years later against New Zealand but it wasn't the same. I had ended my own Test career without one last crack at the Australians – in those days, the prize for all rugby league players. And it was all my own fault.

NINE

The good, the bad and some of the other kind

Thousands of matches spread over more than forty years in the game tend to leave the odd mark or two, a fair share of heroes and villains, and one game that stands out above all the rest. Okay, I have already mentioned it, but it was much more than just another game.

Brisbane 1958 was the venue and date of a match that will forever live in my memory for more than just the heroics of Alan Prescott who played for all but the opening few minutes with a broken arm. This was a game full of quality rugby league played by men who had pride in the jersey they wore. There were no big-money incentives to beat the Australians in those days. What may sound like sentimental old twaddle to the modern player with his six-figure contract and personalised-numberplated car, or the one who can afford to cry off a tour because he has a sore thumb, was in fact the only incentive we ever needed in that generation: pride in what we did.

It had nothing to do with money. On the contrary – a £360 tour fee for three months spent abroad meant that we all lost money. Before we left we had to hold collections among our clubmates to raise the money that would keep us going throughout the tour. We weren't even offered a pair of boots to play in – and woe betide you if you lost a pair of the team's socks because the cost of replacements would be docked off your wages!

My wife Alice summed it up nicely when making comparisons with today's players – she and Mick Sullivan's wife used to dread the sound of the ice-cream van chimes because she couldn't afford to buy a cornet for the kids. And we were branded as rugby outcasts because we were professionals!

It is hard to imagine in these days of unlimited substitutes, of modern, high-tech treatment for injuries, that any team will ever again go through what we had to endure in Brisbane.

Of course, skipper Prescott was the inspiration. With David Bolton already on his way to hospital and three others carrying knocks that today would earn a player a fortnight's lay-off, the mere inconvenience of a broken arm was not going to prevent Prescott leading out his team for the second half. 'We just won't tell anybody. At least I can get in the way and the Aussies will have to run round me to get where they are going,' he said, and at that moment I think we would all have followed him to the end of the world.

But, heroics apart, this was a match of quality rugby league and it ended with Britain's Lions having won over the hearts and minds of the Australian crowd. And don't just take my word for it . . . the Australian press could hardly believe it, headlining the match report: 'BATTLETORN LIONS STEAMROLL AUSTRALIA – Murphy brilliance inspires crippled Englishmen'; in a book published several years later, *Australian Rugby League's Greatest Games: Unforgettable Moments* – the tributes were glowing: 'The Englishmen crumpled like flies in the opening minutes of the game and it seemed only a matter of time before the might of a full-strength Australia would overcome them and wrap up the Test series.

'But it was not to be. Inspired by the brilliance of the elusive Alex Murphy, the bedraggled Englishmen defied the odds and carried off the seemingly impossible. It was an embarrassing time for Australia.'

It still stirs up passion and pride all these years later. The Australian report went on: 'Five minutes after the start of the second Test in Brisbane, English skipper Alan Prescott snapped his right arm. Twelve minutes later England's five-eighth [stand-off] David Bolton broke a collarbone and was led off the field in agony.

'So the scene was set for one of the epic matches in rugby league Test history. England [Great Britain], with Bolton off the field, Prescott playing with a broken arm and three other men in agony with injuries, somehow managed to beat Australia. Inspired by Prescott's courage and the unrivalled brilliance of half-back Alex Murphy, England squared the series, winning the Test 25 points to 18.

'Veteran League men described the victory as a repeat of the famous "Rorke's Drift" Test of 1914 when England, with only ten men on the field, defeated Australia 14–6 to regain the Ashes. And probably only the Rorke's Drift Test could compare in raw courage with what England managed that afternoon in 1958. They played for 63 minutes a man short and with four severely injured players on the field. Undoubtedly it was the courage of their captain Alan Prescott that provided the glowing inspiration for the victory.

'Prescott felt his arm "go" in a tackle in the first few minutes and passed the news on to his teammates. He refused to go off. The injury list grew. Bolton, doubled up with pain, had no choice but to leave the field after breaking a collarbone. Centre Jim Challinor then suffered a severe shoulder injury, which should have seen him off the field. He stayed. So, too, did lock Vince Karalius (injured spine) and full-back Eric Fraser (elbow injury). After the match was over, ambulancemen wrapped the five wounded heroes in blankets and took them to hospital; Prescott and Bolton did not play again on tour.

'At half-time the English dressing-room was like a hospital ward. Team manager Tom Mitchell gave Prescott the choice of retiring or returning to the field of play. Coach Jim Brough told Prescott: "Alan, I want you out there on the field." Prescott unhesitatingly led his men back out into the fray again, playing the match one-handed – handling, passing and tackling with his left hand.

'Centre Challinor needed a painkilling needle to get back on to the field in the second half. But back he went. By rights Australia should have steamrollered England and wrapped up the Ashes in that Test. But it has often been said that an Englishman is at his best when the going gets tough – and that's the way it was on 5 July 1958.

'The Australians played inexplicably poorly. The forwards were loose and let the Englishmen run through them, and the handling was appalling, with players often forfeiting

The young Alex (front row, centre) lines up with his St Austin's school team.

RIGHT: The great man who became a second father to Alex, his coach and mentor Jim Sullivan.

'Kneed' any help? A Huddersfield player (could it really be Peter Ramsden under there?) feels the force of a combined Vollenhoven–Murphy . . . er . . . tackle.

OPPOSITE PAGE: In full flow: Murphy displaying the kicking style that had opponents backpedalling, and on the run for Saints against Widnes.

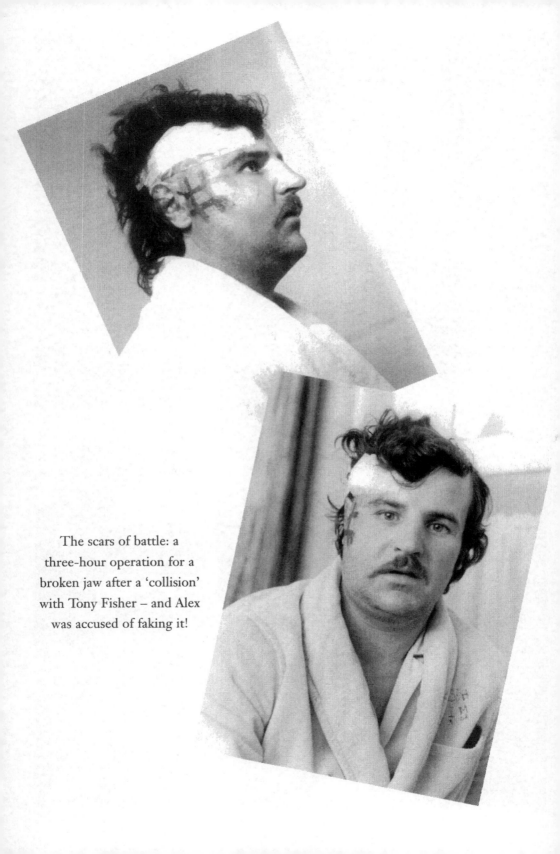

The scars of battle: a three-hour operation for a broken jaw after a 'collision' with Tony Fisher – and Alex was accused of faking it!

ABOVE: Winners (1): Murphy (front row, second left) and his team-mates chair their captain Vince Karalius with the Lancashire Cup.

BELOW: Winners (2): more suits than jerseys! The Saints board join the players to pose with the Challenge Cup and Lancashire Cup (1961).

ABOVE: Murphy descends the Wembley steps with the coveted Challenge Cup after Saints had demolished arch-rivals Wigan.

BELOW: Four cups – but no Murphy! The all-conquering St Helens side of 1966 pose for the official club photograph, but the mercurial Murphy, architect of so much of the success, failed to turn up because of his dispute with the club.

A proud moment: leading out Great Britain for a Test against France.

Wigan players go through their paces on the Southport sands,
a 'training ground' also used by Red Rum.

RIGHT: Shaun Edwards was probably Murphy's finest signing – but,
as his T-shirt proves, he wasn't always the best at everything!

Alex and his wife Alice at the gates of Buckingham Palace for the OBE ceremony.

LEFT: With his OBE for services to the game in the 1999 New Year Honours List.

BELOW: At least he is kind to animals: a lost bird cries on Alex's shoulder.

possession in tackles. The bulldog forwards of England and the dazzling Alex Murphy set up the win which led ultimately to the Ashes victory in the deciding Third Test.

'Murphy, one of the great half-backs of all time, paved the way for England's first four tries and scored the last one. Cheeky, pugnacious, with dazzling speed and supreme football skills, Murphy showed that afternoon why he was subsequently to become regarded as one of the greatest players of them all.

'It was Murphy who got England going only four minutes after the start, when he ran wide from a ruck in midfield and shot down the left flank. Front-rowers Prescott and McTigue linked up and the skilful Brian McTigue positioned Jim Challinor for the try.

'The second try came six minutes before half-time. On this occasion Murphy broke two tackles and spearheaded a raid deep into Australia's 25. Again McTigue was the man who gave the final try-creating pass, this time to winger Mike Sullivan.

'By half-time England had run up a lead of 10–2, but so bad were their injuries that it seemed inevitable that Australia would overrun them in the second half.

'It never looked like happening.

'England consolidated their position with a most important try only three minutes after half-time, set up again by Murphy and scored by winger Ike Southward. Australian front-rower Bill Marsh finally put a try on the board for the home side after fourteen minutes when he barged his way over.

'Marsh was the only Australian forward who played well enough on the day to justify his selection. Others, like Norm Provan, Kel O'Shea and Rex Mossop, were well below par.

Only half-back Keith Holman and five-eighth Tony Brown saved Australia from complete disgrace; both tackled like men inspired, many times plugging up gaps left open by their forwards. Marsh's try got Australia back to 15–7 but the Aussies never looked to have the faintest hope of winning the day.

'The Englishmen shrewdly closed the game up in the closing stages. They resorted to any possible means to waste time, determined to protect their hard-earned lead. Some of the go-slow tactics were so blatant that spectators in the crowd of 32,500 called to referee Darcy Lawler to whistle time-off.

'After Marsh's try, Australia added three to England's two. But it was a forlorn fightback. The day belonged to Alan Prescott and his gallant band of Englishmen. Against all the odds they had achieved the impossible and no league fan who saw the Test will ever forget their bulldog courage that day.'

'Alan Prescott and his gallant band of Englishmen', 'bulldog spirit' – I like that, and coming from an Australian writer, too. Who wouldn't be proud of the part he played in that memorable day? I know I am . . . it is the game I will always remember.

*

While the Brisbane Test is the one that will stick in my memory for ever, it was a year later, in far less dramatic circumstances and away from the glare of Anglo–Aussie Test arenas at Leeds when I scored four tries against France that I got the most personal satisfaction. We won that match 50–15 and it was played in front of a crowd of twenty-two thousand people. These days – and it happened in that hotbed of the game at The Boulevard, Hull, in October 1999 – the same match draws an attendance of barely three thousand.

Among the other games I will always cherish, I suppose, the 1971 Cup final probably ranks high in the memory bank as a match to savour, but I did not realise how good it was until years later when I got round to watching the video.

Roses battles with Yorkshire and the inter-county clashes up in Cumbria – now sadly a thing of the past – were all part and parcel of the part-time rugby league player's season of fifty or more matches. But that Test in Brisbane tops the lot as far as I am concerned and I am sure it will never be repeated. For one thing, there are rows of substitutes waiting to replace anybody who suffers the slightest knock; for another, rugby league is now, by comparison, a clinically clean sport. There is no hiding place for thuggery and skulduggery which were rife before the arrival of the TV camera close-ups and slow-motions.

Although I can single out the Brisbane Test as the best, I would be hard pressed to find the match that I considered the dirtiest – you got them by the barrow-load. There was a very good reason for that: money. Or, more accurately, the lack of it. Winning was everything. It made the difference between having a holiday in Blackpool or the Isle of Man or spending half the summer visiting a local park. And to achieve that trip to enjoy the delights of Skegness or wherever, there were players who would overstep the mark. Fish and chips or bread and dripping? That was the environment of rugby league, the so-called professional sport in those days.

And because of that I make no claims to being an angel. I bent a few noses in my career as well as having my own remodelled a few times. If the coach suggested that it might be a good idea to see that the star of the opposition didn't enjoy himself, well, I was prepared to be a party to that. It was, after all, just a tactic, but I can honestly say I never set out to do anybody any permanent damage.

That is more than you can say for some of the players I came across in the 1970s. It was a period when rugby league was at its wildest – hence the outrageous *Daily Mail* headline of the 1970 World Cup final which demanded 'GET THESE SAVAGES OFF OUR SCREEN' after one particularly nasty game between Great Britain and the Australians when Fred Lindop, the top referee of the time, was forced to break up a succession of fights.

There were indeed some brutal matches and none was much worse than one Boxing Day local derby between my old club Leigh and my new team Warrington, or so I am told – I had already been stretchered off and was lying concussed in the dressing-room when the fireworks really started.

Clearly some of my old teammates were out to prove a point and they set about it in a good old-fashioned way. Brawls and battles broke out all over the pitch, some players were sent off while others were carried off and, all in all, the ten thousand-strong crowd loved every minute of it!

I don't doubt that many of the supporters of the modern game will assume that all this is merely the ramblings of a player from the dinosaur age . . . but the game was tougher, physically harder and, yes, a lot dirtier in those days. I am not for a minute suggesting that is a good thing – it was simply a fact of rugby league life. There was no video evidence to protect you. If the referee or his touch judge didn't see it then the bad guy got away with it. You had to learn to look after yourself – get your retaliation in first.

The game has been cleaned up, almost sanitised, to the point where even the slightest dig cannot go undetected. Something has gone out of rugby league during the clean-up campaign and, while it might suit the modern spectator (though evidence suggests otherwise), it is not a game that the roughneck forwards of the 1960s and 1970s would easily recognise. In an age when winning was everything, polite congratulations and handshaking was for losers. I never wanted to shake anybody's hand if I had lost a match.

And there were places I would rather not have visited on a Saturday afternoon, grounds that, sadly, are no longer part of the game. Toughest of all were the twice-yearly trips up to Cumberland to play Workington and Whitehaven. Draw one of those away in a Challenge Cup tie and you could bet there would be a queue of players round the corner leading to the doctor's surgery, all looking for sicknotes to give the coach. But that wouldn't cut any ice with men like Jim Sullivan – it would take the arrival of a coffin to convince him that you were not fit to make the trip.

And when you got there, the reception was everything you expected. Both grounds were the graveyard of many Cup and League ambitions as Cumbrian pride went to work. At Workington, where they had men like Brian Edgar and the Martin brothers – they all seem like giants compared with some of today's players – the idea was to knock ten bells out of those fancy-dans from St Helens. And, more often than not, they would succeed.

But if a trip to Cumberland was something to be avoided, there was just as much in store once you crossed that *real* border . . . the Pennines. Thrum Hall, Halifax, on a cold November afternoon, a packed crowd baying for blood and the likes of Jack Wilkinson breathing fire and prepared to answer their every wish . . . Or, Watersheddings, Oldham, where it could freeze over in July, and a pack of forwards who could make even Vince Karalius tread carefully . . .

Both these grounds are now no longer. Nor is another of the great gladiatorial arenas, Hull Kingston Rovers' old Craven Park. And there is no more of Hunslet's Parkside where Geoff Gunney reigned supreme . . .

Featherstone's Post Office Road – happily still there but modernised to become the Lionheart Stadium – was another address to put the fear of God into visiting teams.

All these grounds were home to some of the roughest, toughest characters – genuine hard men who protected their own territory. At Warrington we had Mike Nicholas whom I brought up from Aberavon and who turned out to be one of the best signings from the Valleys. He was as tough as they come . . . but it just shows how a person can mellow over the years. Mike, who spent as much time at disciplinary hearings as anybody in the game, has been team manager of Wales for several years and will lead his country into the next World Cup.

Then there was Frank Foster – another fearsome forward who once threatened to tear me limb from limb . . . and that was while we were walking down the tunnel on to the field. Jack Wilkinson really meant it when he tried to kick me over the scrum at Thrum Hall! But one thing all these hatchet-men had in common was that they would happily buy me a drink after spending eighty minutes trying to remove my head from my shoulders.

Among them all, though, there was always one who had a genuine mean streak . . . a player who took great delight in dishing it out. Such a smiling assassin was a Welshman by the name of Tony Fisher. If ever a player could generate evil with a smile it was the former Leeds and Bradford hooker. And I get the feeling he would be more interested in knowing what hospital he could send you to rather than which bar we were heading to for an after-match pint.

When you make it as a top player and become a major influence in the game you expect to be singled out for some special, close attention. I knew that nine out of ten coaches would send out players with the direct instruction to 'Get that little bugger, Murphy!'

I had built up a reputation over the years as a smart alec, a bit of a big mouth and a player who knew how to handle himself. And for that Tony Fisher decided I had to go. I learned the hard way that he was a player I should have learned to give a wide berth. You didn't take liberties with his kind no matter how smart you thought you were. In fact, I believe you had to belong to a different planet to play the game the way Fisher went about his business.

He was one of the hard breed who could never be known by any of the affectionate titles that many of the game's villains could lay claim to. Endearing names like 'loveable rogue' and 'gentle giant' could never apply to Tony Fisher. There were lots of stories about Fisher's tough-guy style, and even when he hung up his boots for the last time, his reputation as a coach was of a man who spread fear wherever he went. On one occasion when he had just taken over as coach at a club, he allowed the backs to go out to start a training session but kept the forwards behind in the dressing-room for what they believed to be a pep-talk. Instead, he turned and locked the door, faced this row of hard-nosed pack men and told them: 'Right – there is only one way out of this dressing-room and that is through that door. And to get through that, first you have to get through me – so let's see how tough you really are!' History does not record the outcome of this famous team talk but I suspect the coach was still standing at the end of it.

My everlasting and painful memory of Fisher came in an important Cup-tie. The match was a Captain Morgan Trophy semi-final against Leeds. The 'rum' trophy was a one-off competition that included the successful teams of the previous season – a nice little earner for some club if you reached the final. Warrington were still on the rise at the time but I knew we had the beating of Leeds even on their own ground.

It was all going to plan and Leeds were becoming more and more frustrated. I intended to keep it that way by turning them with long kicks deep into their territory. It was working a charm when a certain Mr Fisher decided that he had seen enough of this cheeky little upstart. I sent a long forty-yard kick downfield, forcing Leeds to turn again, and we began to chase the ball. Stupid of me, I know, but having sent the ball on its way, I felt I could relax. I lowered my arm from in front of my face – that's a natural defence mechanism when opposing forwards are bearing down on you – and the hit-man from Wales took his chance. Smack! He took me with everything he had and I was sent crashing to the turf. It was a vicious late assault and it came close to ending my career. While the Warrington fans screamed for Fisher to be sent off, referee Mick Naughton, who had missed the incident, consulted his touch judge. After a lengthy discussion, all Warrington got was a penalty. Fisher stayed on because the touch judge thought I was faking it.

The following day I had to undergo a three-and-a-half-hour operation on a jaw that was smashed in three places. Another inch either way, I was told, and I could have been in serious trouble. But the worst part of all was that I believe Tony Fisher actually enjoyed the brutality of it all. We get on well enough these days – another feud that has been healed by time – but if I had to pick one player who went way beyond the bounds of rough play and into the ranks of being a sheer, uncomplicated dirty player who enjoyed causing mayhem just for the hell of it, Tony Fisher was that man.

It was, however, something to put on my CV that Warrington went on to become the one and only winners of the Captain Morgan Trophy.

There are no Fisher-like brutes in the sport these days mainly because the game is covered from every angle by television cameras, videos, in-goal touch judges, in-stand assessors. There is simply no hiding place and the game is almost injury-free. That fact alone is one major change that the clean-up campaigners can hail as a plus.

TEN

The ones that got away . . . and some that didn't

Converts from rugby union – or 'defectors' as the other code was inclined to call them, as though they had committed some heinous, treason-like crime – flooded into the league game during the 1980s. Some made it big, others didn't make it at all, and I had my share of success in the signing market as rugby league tried to lift its profile.

But two of the biggest names to evade the Murphy net were players who would have made their mark in any era. As I have said, one of the things that separates the good from the average and the great from the good is speed . . . and two of the men who made a big impact in recent times had speed to spare.

Martin Offiah was undoubtedly the modern-day winger who could look back on a ten-year career with Widnes and Wigan (his move to London Broncos was nothing more than

a gimmick) with pride. I only wish I could have included the
name St Helens in that list of clubs. Unfortunately, it was not
to be, although I did recommend him to the board.

St Helens, though, have never been a club to rush into
things. Sometimes they have had up to thirteen or fourteen
directors all keen to have their say, and by the time that has
happened the chance has gone. So it was with Offiah. He was
a young lad playing with Rosslyn Park and people were
already talking about him as a future rugby union
international. I put my case to the Saints board and they
thought about it. And thought about it a bit more. Then they
decided that they would send somebody along to watch him
in action. I knew that once they had seen him in action they
would be ready to make him an offer. But the visit, by two
Saints directors, came and went and I heard nothing. So I
asked what was going on and the report came back that the
board had decided, on the evidence of their spying mission,
not to consider Offiah because, although he had speed, he
was an 'unco-ordinated clown'.

Weeks later I sat in the dug-out at Widnes and watched
this clown score three tries against us. My loss was Duggie
Laughton's gain. Duggie, then the Widnes coach, had no
such problems in convincing either his committee or the
player that Naughton Park would be the ideal arena for his
talents. At ten thousand pounds a year on a ten-year contract,
he probably picked up a coach's dream bargain.

Although Offiah got away through the incompetence of a
couple of directors, the same could not be said about another
player who made it right to the top after switching codes. St
Helens did all in their power to sign Jonathan Davies. With
rugby union in Wales struggling to hang on to its star players
in an age when it was still officially amateur, we heard

through the grapevine that the talented Welshman was thinking of moving north to cash in on his skills.

For once, Saints were not slow off the mark and Davies was invited along for talks. He visited director Joe Pickavance's home and we were confident that we could make him an offer he would not be able to refuse.

We tried everything to persuade him to sign but, just like his most famous stand-off predecessor back in the 1950s, Cliff Morgan, he went back to the Valleys without putting pen to paper. Three years later he signed for Widnes and Duggie Laughton had made another scoop from under the noses of Saints. But I am convinced that had Davies joined Saints instead of Widnes he would have been an even better player than he turned out to be for Widnes and Warrington.

Scotsman Alan Tait – who was still strutting his stuff with Scotland in the 1999 rugby union World Cup – was another who elected to join Widnes instead of Saints, as did John Devereux.

But for all those who got away there were others whose signings gave great job satisfaction both at St Helens and, even earlier, at Wigan. I get a bit tetchy when I hear people on the fringe of the game saying 'so-and-so is a good player' after watching him score three tries in a big match. It's a bit like saying 'That Pele can play a bit' while the Brazilians were running riot in a World Cup tie. Anybody can do it.

Players like Dave Chisnall, Ian Potter, Brian Case and Paul Groves may not have become famous enough to make it into the Sunday magazines but they were some of rugby league's steadiest internationals and I am proud to say that I was the man who brought them all into the big time.

But there was one special signing and I believe I am not stretching the imagination when I say that the signing of

Shaun Edwards was not only the best I ever made – he was probably the best *Wigan* ever made! As I had done back in 1955, Shaun put his signature on a contract at midnight on his birthday and from the day he turned seventeen he did his town and his club proud. His father, my old schoolboy partner Jackie, and I set up the deal and I believe that Shaun not only wanted to play for his home-town club, he wanted to play for me. And, for ten years and more, he was the perfect example of the professional rugby league player. He ended up as the most decorated player in the game's history – perhaps I should feel a bit envious – and although his parting from Wigan was not a happy one and he had miserable spells at Bradford Bulls and London Broncos before moving back to London and playing in a Challenge Cup final, Shaun Edwards' heart throbs with cherry-and-white Wigan blood.

I signed Gary Connolly, for long considered to be Britain's best centre, from local club Blackbrook and he eventually left Saints for Wigan for a record quarter-of-a-million pounds.

David Stephenson proved to be an excellent signing from Fylde rugby union club – even though he was hardly the most enthusiastic of trainers and a broken fingernail would prompt a rush to the surgery for a doctor's note.

And Stuart Ferguson, a winger from Wales, may not have been a headline-hugging name but he could kick goals for fun and Leigh would not have made it all the way to Wembley without his boot.

Naturally, not every player I signed was an instant – or even slow-burning – success. One such player who moved north during the boom time for converts was Welsh prop Stuart Evans. I felt sorry for Stuart – he really wanted to make a go of it in rugby league but it simply wasn't going to happen. I remember the day he signed and he was introduced to the press. A giant of a man who had just come back from a Lions tour, his shape and size raised a few eyebrows and knowing nudges from the gathering of reporters.

'Don't worry,' I told them all. 'He'll be fine when he sheds a couple of stone.'

What I didn't say to them – but I did tell Stuart – was 'You are going to have to lose a couple of stone before you can even start training to play this game, son.'

Sadly, it never happened for the lad, although I will argue that, on his day, Stuart Evans was as good a prop as we had in the game at the time. Nobody liked to play against him and his enthusiasm knew no limits. It's just that he was never mobile enough for rugby league but it was not through a want of trying.

Being a coach or a team manager means you don't really have to think about the money side of the club. That is the directors' business so when I missed out on the likes of Jonathan Davies and Martin Offiah I just had to shrug my shoulders and get on with it. But Stuart Evans had cost Saints something like eighty thousand pounds and, not to put too fine a point on it, was a signing that backfired on me. I wasn't allowed to forget it for a long time.

Not quite so expensive was another Welshman who definitely didn't live up to my expectations. Danny Harris was known as the Man Mountain, the hardest man ever to come north from Wales. When he came into the club boardroom at Leigh we had visions of having to raise the ceiling to get him inside. I could see this six-foot six-inch monster spraying the opposition all over the field with barnstorming runs followed by countless tries as the backs took advantage of the mayhem he had caused in the opposing ranks. Some vision! I think I managed to get two good games out of the big guy before he was laid out by a little half-back. I knew then I had trouble.

But, over the years, I think my stock is in credit. I did not let too many world-class players pass me by.

*

One club where I didn't even come close to missing out on a world-class player – let alone signing one – was Salford. My move to the Willows, where the fans have to live forever in the shadow of Manchester United a few miles down the road, was the biggest disaster of my career. I was, not to put too fine a point on it, sold down the river.

I had enjoyed success at Leigh and Warrington – nine trophies in ten years without too much money to spend on players – but in May 1978, only a few months after I had led Warrington to their second John Player Trophy victory in my stay at Wilderspool, the time had come to move on.

The end at Warrington came following rumours and counter-rumours that Ossie Davis and Brian Pitchford were about to leave the club. I had also heard stories that they were not going to renew my contract.

For once, I didn't face the problem head on; but when Albert White, a close friend and chief scout at Warrington, moved out and on to the Salford board, he told me he had only accepted if there was room for me as club coach.

The way things were going at Warrington, the time for a change seemed right. And Salford appeared to be the perfect stopping-off place for a coach with ambition.

They say you live and learn in all walks of life and it didn't take long for me to discover that Salford and Alex

Murphy was never going to be a marriage made in heaven.

The club had enjoyed the heady success of two First Division titles in 1974 and 1976 and their line-up in those seasons looked like a *Who's Who* of rugby's glamour names. They were known through the League as the Quality Street Gang. Household names such as David Watkins, Keith Fielding, Maurice Richards, Mike Coulman and Colin Dixon had all served the club with distinction after switching in big-money deals from rugby union. Add to those such well-established rugby league stars as Chris Hesketh, Ken Gill, Steve Nash and Eric Prescott, and you get some idea of the quality that Salford supporters had become used to over the years. Hence the team's nickname.

I arrived at the Willows full of ambition and enthusiasm, but that was soon to disappear as I learned that my success at Leigh and Warrington was something of a cross to bear.

Maybe I was expecting too much. I thought I was joining a club eager for a return to the glory days, a club who would provide the money I needed to sign the players I wanted. I was living in false hope. The players who had given the club their two titles were all growing old together and the coaching seat had been occupied by Colin Dixon (for ten months) and Stan McCormick (one month) since the departure of Les Bettinson in March 1977. By the time I arrived, Salford were a club looking to rebuild. It was a challenge I relished and one I knew I could handle if . . .

It turned out to be the biggest *if* in my career.

Salford were owned by Brian Snape, a millionaire who, I thought, would have money to spend bringing more glory to the club and replace that Quality Street Gang whose good days were well behind them. The club was used to having superstars – flying Keith Fielding even won the TV event of that name – so I did not anticipate any problems. It was only when I went to ask for money to spend that the truth hit me. Salford wanted the glory back, sure, but they wanted it back without spending a penny.

Brian Snape went off to live in tax exile on the Isle of Man and left the club affairs in the hands of his brother Keith. Now, although Keith was a nice bloke and we got on well, he hardly had the clout needed to open the purse-strings. Every decision was made in a phone call to the Isle of Man and it was perfectly clear that our owner in exile had no intention of spending any cash. The attitude appeared to be: 'Murphy won things with Leigh and Warrington without any money – why does he need it now? Can't he go out and find players?'

It felt like a deliberate policy to prevent me succeeding . . . as if Brian Snape was saying: 'See what we achieved – now let's see how good you really are without my money to help you.'

From day one my hands were tied behind my back. My stay at the Willows was a disaster. The players, who were used to being allowed to swan around and enjoy their super-star status, did not take too kindly to being told what to do by Murphy. On top of that, Brian Snape treated the club like some kind of private toy or hobby and there was nothing anybody could do about it.

After two seasons and two months with the club I was on my way back to Leigh in November 1980. That season Salford were relegated to the Second Division and although I felt sorry for the people I had left behind – Kevin Ashcroft was the man who took over – I wasn't the least bit surprised. Even in those far-off days before full-time professionalism and BSkyB's TV millions of pounds, you could not treat a club as though it was a toy.

On one occasion when the going got tough, I had to face

up to a threatened strike from the players, many of whom did not like my way of doing things. I tried to bring discipline where there had been a lackadaisical attitude to things such as training times, dress codes and so on. It may have come as a bit of a culture shock to a set of players who had let things slide but I had been brought in to do a job and I was going to give it my best effort – even if some people didn't approve. One of the issues they raised when they threatened to go on strike was my use of industrial language! Swearing at them, for heaven's sake! But, once they had had their say, a strike was averted and they got on with the business of playing rugby.

But it was never going to be another Leigh or Warrington. Barely two and a half years into my contract I decided to leave Salford. The playing record had improved and the club became a top-four side and made good progress in the knock-out competitions without actually smashing any pots, but I was getting nowhere. So, towards the end of 1980, during a trip to Yorkshire, I decided the time had come to move on. But I was determined that I was going to give them something to remember me by – so I handed in my resignation halfway through a game at Wakefield Trinity.

I had tried once before to jack it all in but had been persuaded by Albert White to stay on. This time Albert was away on a scouting mission so I handed my letter of resignation to my assistant coach Frank Wilson in the dug-out at Wakefield and asked him to deliver it to the chairman up in the stand.

This time the resignation was accepted and there was a parting of the ways. No tears were shed, there were no sob stories about how things might have worked out, if only . . . the parting was, I suspect, a relief all round.

Salford paid the price, not of taking a chance on Alex

Murphy, but of neglect at the top. And now grandly renamed Salford City Reds, they are still treading water after more than two decades during which time their only rewards have been two Second Division championship titles. Hardly a success story for a club who once had everything but threw it all away. In the next ten years they got through six coaches and they still under-achieved. And, they still are.

What a contrast to Leigh who expected nothing and ended up on top of the rugby league world. I was glad to be back at Hilton Park only a few days after I left Salford.

ELEVEN

Hi, Leigh (again) . . . and Wigan . . . and St Helens

My abrupt departure from Salford soon had the tongues wagging and the newspapers speculating. Two days after quitting, I was spotted at Hilton Park watching Leigh play the Kiwi tourists, and that was enough to get the fans talking and the local press wondering if I was planning a quick return to my old job. A fortnight later I was back at the helm.

Nearly ten years down the line things had changed a lot at Leigh. Brian Bowman was the chairman; John Stringer was the secretary and the board consisted of a few faces I didn't know. One of them was Bobby Hope, a Blackpool entrepreneur who was keeping an eye on the club's finances. I first crossed swords with him over an expenses claim.

It was common practice for coaches to have their telephone bills paid by the club and at Leigh there had never been any problem in the past. But having submitted mine –

along with an electricity bill – I was summoned before the board when Bobby Hope challenged me for an explanation. I started to tell him about it but he interrupted me: 'No, no, I'm not talking about the phone bill. That's fine, we'll pay that – but we're not paying your electricity bill as well.'

I looked him straight in the eye: 'Surely you don't expect me to make all my phone calls in the dark!'

I still don't know whether he thought I was being serious but he must have liked my cheek. The bills got paid.

Although Leigh was still a small-town club in the shadow of big brother Wigan, there was no shortage of talent at Hilton Park on my return. Des Drummond, who went on to play more than twenty times for Great Britain, was a deadly winger on his day, and Steve Donlan, who also toured with the Lions, was in the centre.

But the outstanding prospect was local boy John Woods. The only person who did not realise just how good a player Woods could be was the lad himself. There was something about lads from Leigh – it's probably still a trait – but they are the most unassuming lot who, although not suffering from an actual inferiority complex, won't go out of their way to give themselves a push. That was John Woods. He was all class whether we played him at stand-off, in the centre or at full-back. And could he kick goals. His handling skills were second to none, he had speed and a sidestep – he was a dream of a player who could have gone on to great things. Instead, he spent most of his career with his home-town club although he did have spells at nearby Warrington and further afield at Bradford. He toured with Great Britain in 1984 and could have gone abroad again four years later but said it was time to give younger players a chance. That was typical of the lad.

I got a great reception from the Leigh fans and within twelve months we had another trophy to show off – the Lancashire Cup was won when we beat star-studded Widnes 8–3 at Wigan. It was Leigh's first trophy since that Wembley win ten years earlier.

But it was only the start. We got on a roll, winning a dozen games on the trot – including a victory at Wigan's fortress Central Park – and as the season neared its climax Leigh were in the hunt to win the Championship for the first time in seventy-six years.

It all hinged on the final match – a trip to bottom-of-the-table Whitehaven. They were already relegation certainties so there was talk of the game being a mere formality. I had been to Whitehaven too many times before, however, to think that all we had to do was turn up.

About three thousand Leigh fans made the trip up the M6 and when we stopped for a light meal at a service station we were swamped with good-luck messages from travelling fans. I was just a bit nervous about Whitehaven. They had a scrum-half called Arnold 'Boxer' Walker, a tiger of a kid who didn't know the meaning of the word surrender (as well as hundreds of other words, I suspect). My right-hand man, Colin Clarke, and I knew we had the players to do the job but we also knew Walker was a danger.

Nothing is ever straightforward in sport and that night at the Recreation Ground was no exception. At half-time we were trailing 4–1 and playing like a bunch of novices. When the whistle blew for the interval the players started to run towards the corner (the dressing-rooms were outside the ground and that's where the half-time cup of tea would be waiting). I had to do something and I had to think fast. Before the players could cover the first ten yards to the security of the dressing-room, I called them back. Heads bowed, they trooped over in my direction. Behind me was a small, delapidated wooden stand that was packed with supporters of the home team who were quick to sneer with jibes such as: 'Come on, Murphy – you're supposed to be champions.' And: 'What's wrong, Leigh – too tough for you up here in Cumbria?'

I took the players beneath that creaking old stand and I let fly. If the Salford players had been upset by my language, it's a good thing they were not at Whitehaven that particular night. I shouted, I bawled, I threatened, I cajoled and coaxed, but above all I appealed. I appealed on behalf of the three thousand supporters who had made the journey north. 'They have paid good money to come and see you lot play here tonight – and this is how you repay them! You've got the chance to make rugby league history tonight and look at you!'

I am sure I must have used up the entire ten minutes' interval time and I am certain that every spectator within a hundred yards of that stand must have heard every word I said. Luckily, it worked. We got on top and once we had scored our first try there was no looking back. We ran in twenty points, Whitehaven and Boxer Walker faded from the scene and we left the Recreation Ground that night as rugby league Division One champions.

I discovered later that, among the after-match interviews given by the players, the one given by Steve Donlan stayed in the minds of all the reporters who were there. 'What was the difference in the second half?' Steve was asked.

'You must have heard it – that half-time talk. The boss said that if we lost this game he would personally fill us in. Either one at a time or all together. And he bloody meant it, too.

With a threat like that hanging over us, we just had to win.'

It was that championship victory that convinced me that I still had something to offer. If I could take Leigh to a title they had hardly dared even dream about then I must have been doing something right. I still had a part to play in rugby league. Within weeks I was in demand by the two biggest clubs in the game and, although I had never really intended to leave Leigh for a second time, the offers that came along were too good to refuse. It was just a matter of deciding which one to take.

*

The first people to knock on my door were the directors of my first love, St Helens. Nearly sixteen years had passed since I left the club under a cloud and had made my mark in the coaching business. Now they were in my house offering me the chance to make a return to Knowsley Road. I was tempted, stirred by memories of the good times I had had during my ten years at the club in the 1950s and 1960s, and I agreed to think it over, knowing in my heart that I wanted to take the job.

But then came the moment that was to change my life in rugby league forever. The next person on my doorstep was none other than Maurice Lindsay who had with him the Wigan chairman Jack Hilton. They had come to make me *that* offer – the one you can't refuse. A job had recently become vacant at Wigan with the sacking of Maurice Bamford after just one year in charge, a year in which Wigan had finished in the bottom half after their return from the Second Division under George Fairbairn (who, in turn, had been sacked to make way for Bamford).

Whatever his faults, Maurice Lindsay is a very persuasive man and I did not need too much convincing when he said: 'Come and join us and we will make Wigan a great club again.'

I ignored the advice of friends that it would all end in tears and I threw in my lot with Wigan and Maurice. And for two years we sowed the seeds for what was to become the most successful club in the history of the game, winning the League and Cup double six times on the trot in the 1990s. No doubt coaches Graham Lowe and John Monie will be the names on everybody's lips when it comes to handing out praise for such achievements. And Lindsay, too, will be able to bask in the reflected glory of such unprecedented success.

But 'that cocky little bugger from St Helens' did more than his share to put Wigan on the road to fame and fortune that spread over the next ten years until the arrival of summer rugby and Super League. The Wigan I joined in June 1982 was a far cry from the Wigan I left behind ready to reap the benefits of the groundwork two years later. For a start, crowds were around the four-thousand mark, the club had spent a season getting out of the Second Division (they finished second under George Fairbairn) and when Bamford brought in players who clearly were not up to the job of taking Wigan to the top, he was given the sack and they sent for me.

There was a massive rebuilding job to do. Wigan had not won the Cup since 1965 or the Championship since 1960, and for a town steeped in the game that state of affairs was something that couldn't go on for much longer. The rugby-loving public had reached the end of their patience – they wouldn't put up with more failure. Second best wasn't good enough so third rate had no chance!

'How do we turn Wigan into a great team?' That was Maurice's first question, and the answer probably seems simple enough now – especially in the light of what happened once I had served my purpose and he had seen me off.

But I told him: 'Go out and buy the best players around.'

Of course, that didn't happen – at least not while I was there. Later he gave Bradford Northern eighty thousand pounds and two internationals for Ellery Hanley – a player I desperately wanted to take to Central Park; he brought in the likes of Brett Kenny and Gene Miles from Australia, and Frano Botica to kick goals for fun; Martin Offiah to score tries; and he went on spending the kind of money that was beyond my wildest dreams as I tried to rebuild Wigan.

I had to make potential champions or cup-winners out of people like Mark Cannon, Wayne Elvin and the Harley-Davidson-riding Kerry Hemsley, he of the flowing locks and the image way beyond the talent – hardly household names or expensive superstars from Down Under to spread fear throughout any opposition.

I did manage to get Shaun Edwards, but he was only a teenager at the time so somebody else would benefit once he had blossomed into the great player he was to become.

Wigan eventually bought their way to the top, going full-time before any other club, but in 1982 they were just another mid-table run-of-the-mill side who had fallen on hard times.

There had been a big shake-up behind the scenes, an unwieldly ten-man board being replaced by Lindsay and three others. Once described as 'a sick club' by my old minder Vince Karalius while he was in charge, something drastic was needed to turn things around.

It wasn't going to happen overnight but by the end of my

first season Wigan had a trophy in their cabinet. A crowd of twenty thousand turned up at Leeds United's Elland Road ground to see Wigan end an eighteen-year famine. We beat Leeds 15–4 with tries from Henderson Gill and my first signing, Brian Juliff.

In addition, we finished third in the First Division, attendances had risen from a meagre four thousand to seven thousand-plus so by the standards set over the previous dozen years or so we had had a season of outstanding success.

The following season Wigan were back at Wembley, to face Widnes. We flew in Hemsley, now back in Australia with Balmain, for the final and we had an overseas contingent that included New Zealand's captain Graeme West, fellow Kiwi Howie Tamati, and Hemsley, Cannon and Elvin from Australia. At full-back was teenager Shaun Edwards.

A travelling army of thirty thousand Wigan fans brought back memories of the good old days, but the club's first Wembley appearance for fourteen years was to end the same way as the previous one . . . in bitter disappointment. *Rothman's Yearbook* tells the story like this: 'Antipodeans Graeme West – the tallest player to appear in a Wembley final at 6ft 5in – Howie Tamati, substitute Wayne Elvin and Hemsley concentrated on one-man rugby. At half-back Gary Stephens buzzed around without ever stinging and Australian Mark Cannon failed to fire. Wigan's only real progress was by Mick Scott in the second row.

'Cannon's first notable contribution to a lacklustre opening period was an ill-judged kick on the half-hour which was deflected to Widnes forward Gorley, who fed Tamati for the ball to be handed on to the quicksilver Lydon for a majestic sprint to the line, Burke again adding a goal. The 1984 final was over as a contest at that point. After the interval Steve O'Neill scooped over his third drop-goal of the competition before Lydon's second try, to be ranked among the all-time great touchdowns at Wembley. In the 71st minute the Great Britain international swooped on a loose ball, cut between two defenders and swerved round the full-back before sprinting clear of the crossfield cover. With four minutes left, Hemsley, hesitating at first, finally decided to use his power and, despite the attentions of three Widnes players, crashed over for Wigan's only try.'

So Wigan had been beaten by Joe Lydon, Wigan born and bred, who would later join his home-town club – who would have to pay £100,000 for allowing him, like so many others, to slip through their scouting net. In the Wigan camp, the disappointment cut deep and the final was a let-down. But I told Maurice at the time: 'Don't worry, Wigan will be back next year.'

I was right about that. The only trouble was I wasn't to be part of it. The bitter parting of the ways came after a summer in which I had thought about the future and how Wigan were heading for the summit again. Their victory over Hull at Wembley in 1985 was the start of their long run of success. But it is worth noting that, in place of unknown Mark Cannon, Wigan now had the world's greatest stand-off in Brett Kenny; and on the wing local product Dennis Ramsdale had been replaced by evergreen Aussie John Ferguson. Steve Donlan, another Test player, had been added to the centres.

Is it any wonder that I got the message that Maurice Lindsay was storing up all my ideas for the day I walked out of the ground for the last time as coach? Or am I expected to believe that it was just coincidence that all the best-laid plans of the Murphy–Lindsay partnership eventually came to fruition almost as soon as the partnership had been dissolved?

*

That sacking by Wigan was probably my darkest hour but, after keeping in touch with the game via radio and television work, I was invited back to Leigh – not to win cups and medals this time but try to stop the ship sinking. But this time it was too late – there were no miracles left in the locker. Leigh were never to get out of the bottom four and were relegated.

The following season wasn't too bad, however. When I left in November they were top of the league and heading for a quick return to the First Division – something they achieved by suffering only one League defeat in their thirty matches. Of course, I was not around to join in the celebrations this time. I was employed elsewhere.

They say that opportunity only knocks once . . . happily for me that is only a saying. Nearly twenty years after I had walked out of Knowsley Road following a bitter dispute, I was back as coach. I had turned down St Helens' offer so that I could go to Wigan so, to all intents and purposes, I had slammed the door on the chances of a return to my home-town club. Then, when I went back to Leigh for the third time, the St Helens job was the last thing on my mind. I was coaching Lancashire at the time when the call came that they wanted to replace Billy Benyon.

You might think it was an easy decision to make – a return to the club where I had played for ten years; where I had learned under the master Jim Sullivan; and to the arch rivals of Wigan, of course, the club from where I had been so unceremoniously dumped. It all added up to the perfect challenge.

But I had my doubts before eventually agreeing to bury the hatchet and return to Knowsley Road.

The welcome hardly represented the sort of homecoming script I would have chosen to write for myself. There was talk of unrest in the dressing-rooms, of players loyal to the previous régime refusing to play for me, and on top of that the team suffered a run of defeats that were an embarrassment to a club with Saints' pedigree.

I decided to tackle the rumours head-on: I invited anybody unwilling to play for me to leave the dressing-room and get out of the club. Nobody did. But it didn't end there and the defeats continued until, after one particularly bad loss at the hands of Bradford Northern, there was another showdown – this time with chairman Lawrie Prescott present. A second clear-the-air talk confirmed that Murphy's Law would apply in all matters relating to the coaching side of the club.

Again the invitation went out for players to leave if they wanted. Again there were no takers. Happily, the players did not need to be told a third time and things started to pick up from that point on. Deep down, however, even though we were on track again, I knew it would take time to get things right.

The following season Saints were back in the serious business of chasing honours, with the Challenge Cup again high on the target list. Despite a dodgy start (a narrow win over Swinton in the preliminary round), Saints made it all the way to Wembley for their first visit for eight years – and more than a quarter of a century after I had made my playing début there in the 1961 final victory over Wigan.

This time the opposition were Halifax, one of the most

impressive clubs of the 1980s, whose team was packed with Australians. Returning to Wembley for the seventh time as player and coach proved to be both uplifting and depressing all in one day. It was great to see the smiling St Helens fans back enjoying the big time. But when it was all over I could hardly believe we had lost. We were trailing by just one point, 19–18, having come back from twice being ten points behind, when our New Zealand centre Mark Elia, who had already scored one try, crossed the Halifax line only to have the ball knocked from his grasp by John Pendlebury. All he had to do was fall down with the ball in his grasp and the Cup would have been ours. At the after-match press conference I said it was like robbing the bank and then throwing the money all over the floor on the way out.

But there was more to the defeat than just that missed chance. As a player I knew the importance of the drop-goal – Jim Sullivan had drummed it into me – and I'd made the St Helens players practise it all week before the final, so I could hardly believe that we didn't try it once. Because in the end, it was a drop-goal – by that man Pendlebury – that won the Cup for Halifax.

As a player, I used the drop-goal whenever it presented itself as an alternative to trying to barge my way through rows of muscle between myself and the try line. And I have it on good authority that the powers-that-be felt that my expertise was winning too many matches when tries – then worth three points – should be the main object of the game. So in 1974 the drop-goal's value was halved to one point. I remember receiving a telephone call from *Manchester Evening News* reporter Jack McNamara who told me of the rule change and asked me what I thought of the alteration. I only had to think for a minute: 'It just means that I will have to drop twice as many,' I told him. What I would have given for even a one-point drop-goal in the Challenge Cup final of 1987.

Less than a year later the trophy cabinet was no longer bare – we had lifted the Regal Trophy (John Player). But there was one major and everlasting disappointment waiting round the corner before I was finally to leave St Helens. It came in the 1989 Challenge Cup final . . . and for the second time the club I was coaching paid to fly over their short-term Australian imports for the final, just as Wigan had done with Kerry Hemsley in 1984. They needn't have bothered. Michael O'Connor and Paul Vautin were Test players with reputations for being the men for the big occasions. They both left those reputations outside the Twin Towers.

For the first time in thirty-eight years a team failed to score a single point in a Wembley Cup final. And that team was St Helens, who were shattered 27–0 by Wigan. It was a humbling and humiliating experience and it's hardly an earth-shattering revelation to divulge who carried the can.

Vautin went back to Australia, publicly rubbished me and the coaching methods at St Helens and blamed the defeat on anybody and everything but himself. And all this from the captain. I just wonder whether he could look in the mirror and say that none of it was his fault.

As a commentator noted at the time: 'The £20,000 exercise of flying back from Sydney the Manly duo Michael O'Connor and Paul Vautin – captain of the day – proved to be an expensive flop as neither Australian Test man made any impact on the committed Wigan rearguard.'

It was a huge disappointment and the recriminations spread far and wide but, in the end, it is the coach who pays the ultimate price. Despite two Wembley visits, a John

Player Trophy victory and an appearance in the Premiership final, by January 1990 the love affair was over and my coaching stint at St Helens was over. By March I was back at Leigh to attempt another salvage job on the relegation-bound club. We stopped the rot in the Second Division, finishing fifth, but in August I left the club for the last time and was about to embark on the sort of job nobody could believe Alex Murphy would ever take on. Across the Pennines. In Yorkshire. And trying desperately to lay to rest ghosts from the past. It was one of the most heartening experiences of my career.

TWELVE

Ghosts from a golden age

A crowd of 32,912 once squeezed themselves on to the terraces for a match against Wigan; the grandstand had housed dignitaries and VIPs from all walks of life; the ground itself had been the stage for a world-record rugby league score that was to survive for more than eighty years; it had been the home of some of greatest players and finest champions in the history of rugby league. Out back, cricketing heroes of Yorkshire had thrilled packed crowds on their regular visits to the famous old ground. Further away, the scenery was stunning – you could not have asked for a finer sporting setting anywhere in the country. Yet, by the time I arrived, those terraces were a crumbling field of weeds and nettles and protected only by rusting iron railings; the stand, condemned and decaying, was held together only by its most recent coat of paint; the cricket square was a five-a-side football pitch and had long since said its last farewell to any cricketer of note. As for the scenery . . . well, nobody really noticed.

That was my introduction to the next stop on my journey through rugby league. It had been the birthplace of the sport nearly a hundred years earlier and by the look of things the club was still living on the memories.

Huddersfield had fallen on hard times. The club had flirted with the gimmicks such as silly nicknames that were later to become the hallmark of Super League in the late 1990s. In 1984 the club had changed the name of its famous ground from Fartown to Arena 84 and the name of its team to Huddersfield Barracudas. On top of that, they had re-titled the reserves Huddersfield Piranhas. No kidding, that was their idea of moving up in the world.

Of course, it didn't work and, when the club hit rock bottom, they sent for Murphy.

It was in September, a couple of weeks after the start of the new season when Dave Parker, a Huddersfield journalist who was also the secretary of the club, talked me into my first venture across the Pennines. It was there that I learned what grass-roots rugby league and its people were all about. My own memories of Huddersfield were of the days when my father used to take me to see them with the promise: 'You are going to see the finest team that ever played this game . . . and probably the greatest you will ever see. They have won everything there is to win – five cups in one season in their heyday – and they have had on their books some of the finest players who have ever played the game.'

That was not the Huddersfield Dave Parker persuaded me to throw in my lot with after my departure from St Helens. But it was there that I came across some of the nicest, most genuine people it has ever been my privilege to meet and work alongside.

As well as Dave himself, the club had a board who were the

salt of the earth – working guys who were determined to see Huddersfield back in the big time. Joe Bramley, Jim Collins and the former St Helens and Barrow forward Mick Murphy (no relation) were the men in charge. Board meetings were a bit delicate but if I asked for money to sign a player, I knew where it came from – they all used to dig deep into their own pockets.

The people of Huddersfield do not realise how much they owe to the likes of Dave Parker for keeping the club alive. Anybody who will mortgage his own house to keep a rugby club afloat with no possible means of ever getting his money back deserves to have a statue built in his honour. And even now, all these years later, I understand Dave is still paying off the bank loan he took out to secure Huddersfield's future.

If he knew then what he knows now – that his successors would sell the club down the river in a so-called merger to save their own positions and give the town a phoney club under the artificial title of Huddersfield–Sheffield Giants – I am certain he would have thought twice. But then our paths would never have crossed and I would not have been reminded of the depth of feeling that rugby league gives to somebody born into the sport.

So, the Huddersfield at which I arrived was far different from the claret-and-golds of a bygone age. This was the club that swept all before them in the years just prior to the First World War, winning cups, leagues and county championships as if it was their right. In the late 1920s and early '30s they were the team of all talents, and the history of rugby league is littered with achievements of some of the club's greats. For the first thirty years of the breakaway from rugby union Huddersfield's history is full of great names – including the prince of centres, Harold Wagstaff, captain of the Great Britain Tourists of 1914 and 1920.

Even though he was well before my time I'm sure I would have liked Wagstaff. Described by a writer of the day as 'a man with a scheming brain that made him the player he was and he had knowledge of the weaknesses of the opposition that gave him the intuition to do the right thing at the right moment', he sounds like my kind of player.

Just like I was, he was signed from the local amateur game but he got even less than I did – a signing-on fee of just five pounds when he joined Huddersfield in November 1906. He wasn't even sixteen years old. Wagstaff's finest hour was to be repeated in Brisbane in July 1958 – forty-four years after the original Rorke's Drift Test.

The story goes that Wagstaff, the tour captain, was upset by an Australian order to play the third Test of the series only five days after the second, having already given in to the request to play two matches in three days. He was not happy and informed the authorities – then the Northern Rugby Union – in England. Back came the message: 'Play match as Australians desire. England expects that every man will do his duty.'

So, under protest, Wagstaff led his team out for the third Test in eight days. Crippled by injuries, they were reduced to ten men inside fifty minutes. But such was the Wagstaff leadership that Britain came through the Test 14–6 to win the series.

Wagstaff, a fellow member of rugby league's exclusive Hall of Fame, was just one of the legends of Huddersfield; Albert Rosenfeld, whose record of eighty tries in one season in 1914 will never be beaten, was another. And in 1954 Scotsman Dave Valentine skippered Great Britain's rank outsiders to victory in the first-ever World Cup. The walls of the supporters' club at Fartown are covered in photographs and cartoons of such great players.

When I arrived, the club hadn't won a major trophy (apart from the Second Division title) since their 1962 Cup final win at Wembley. I was the twenty-first coach in fifteen years. It was not what you could call a club of stability. As I sat in the stand that was about to fall apart and looked out towards the weeds and nettles and the scoreboard that would not survive another strong wind, I had visions of the ghosts of Rosenfeld and Wagstaff ripping through the opposition.

One constant, though, was the groundsman Frank Doyle. He remembered players like Dave Valentine, Ken Bowman, Frank Dyson and Don Close – all internationals from the last time Huddersfield were a serious rugby league club. And at the same time there was a teenage winger who would eventually become one of my closest friends and the most capped player in the game – Mick Sullivan. By 1990 the club was fighting a losing battle. But Frank was a groundsman of the old school and, as such, I knew I had to get on the right side of him. He wouldn't give away as much as a pair of boot laces to the present crop of players let alone clean their boots. And when it came to training on his precious pitch, he wasn't slow in barking out the orders to keep off the grass. So my first job was to get on his good side. We had a lot in common and we both believed that the game's greatest days were when you had to earn respect; when heroes rubbed shoulders with the man in the street and had no edge. The 'old school'. We got on famously and I appreciated everything he was doing for the club – even to the extent that the players were not wasting the soap he was putting in the baths.

Once I had won Frank over I used to sit alone in the old stand and stare out across the pitch and wonder how the hell I was going to entice the crowds back to the famous old ground. Two victories – at Nottingham City and one-season wonders Scarborough Pirates – were followed by a home defeat at the hands of Batley and then wins against Ryedale-York and Bramley. It was not a bad start but, remember, the famous old claret-and-golds were now down in the Third Division so it was hardly headline-grabbing stuff.

On 25 September 1991 I took up Dave Parker's offer and, after recruiting former Oldham and Great Britain loose-forward Terry Flanagan as my assistant, I moved in at run-down Fartown.

The first night was unbelievable. Huddersfield, who by now had dropped the Barracudas from their title, had been drawn at home to First Division Wakefield Trinity – in their pre-Wildcat days – in the second round of the Yorkshire Cup. The kick-off had to be delayed to allow the crowd of close on five thousand – more than three times the expected turn-out – into the ground.

Of course, it was no fairytale victory to launch my stay at Huddersfield, but even a 52–9 defeat could not dampen my enthusiasm for the job. With Dave Parker at my shoulder it was impossible to feel down for long. He and the directors were working to keep the great old club alive and he wanted me to be part of it.

Soon we were visiting just about every factory in the Huddersfield area, begging and borrowing anything we could to help the club. On one occasion, Dave and I went to Halifax to perform the ceremony of opening a shop and get some publicity by arranging for the owner to let off hundreds of balloons before one of our home games. When I asked our intrepid secretary what this bloke did for the club, he replied: 'He supplies us with all our soap.' Sponsorship on a grand scale, but it had to be done.

Just as the supporters' club arranged hot-pot suppers, bingo nights and car-boot sales, so Dave and I scoured the district for local businessmen who would be prepared to put money into the club. This was all about keeping a famous institution alive, and if everybody in the town could have matched the pride in the club that Dave Parker showed we would have been on Easy Street.

On the pitch things were picking up, although a slip-up at Batley didn't help our race to the top. One of the season's highlights was a visit from St Helens in the Regal Trophy when, once again, Fartown buzzed with a crowd of over four thousand. We were far from disgraced in going down 32–10.

But the benchmark for our improvement came when we were drawn to visit Wakefield Trinity in the Challenge Cup. Wakefield had whipped us 52–9 on my first day in charge. This time they scraped home by four points. By the end of the season Huddersfield were back among the trophies as Third Division champions. A year later, in the Second Division, we finished third, just one spot off another promotion and a place among the élite. But a reorganisation of the league – they seemed to happen and go on happening every year – condemned the club to a place downstairs.

But that wasn't the worst news. Before that, the battle for survival had been getting tougher and the administrator was called in. It was a new experience for me to sit in an office and be told by an outsider that we had to sell all the players to stay in business. Even worse, I had to persuade the supporters' club to find the funds to pay for a coach and an overnight stay at Whitehaven. The club survived and ten straight wins at the start of the 1993–94 season took Huddersfield up among the big shots of the Second Division.

But it couldn't last. There were changes behind the scenes, the season ended with the club in fifth place in Division Two and the greatest adventure of my coaching career was over. There had been some great times along the way – and even the Jockey Club had a say in the club's publicity machine. As joint owners of a racehorse we wanted to name it after the club's famous ground – Fartowner – but the Jockey Club objected . . . on the grounds of taste! So the horse became Claret And Gold – the club colours.

My trip into Yorkshire gave me the chance to work with some great rugby league people like Mike Murphy and Dave Parker; I wonder if they feel as sad as I do about the state of the game in the town in this golden age of Super League. Who would have thought that only four years after leaving the rundown home for the luxurious surroundings of the new McAlpine Stadium the club would be on its knees again. Even with Rupert Murdoch's millions they have managed to get themselves into a mess that has resulted in a merger with Sheffield Eagles. Crowds went down to three thousand and all the dancing girls and cuddly mascots in the world have been unable to generate the sort of atmosphere that made Fartown and Huddersfield favourites. Fartown is still the name on the lips of the Huddersfield-Sheffield Giants as the new millennium begins.

And to think that the town bearing the name of the birthplace of rugby league almost went missing from the fixture lists. In the meantime, Dave Parker and Mike Murphy are still trying to pay off the debts that kept the club alive in its darkest hours while today's candyfloss powers-that-be have only to snap their fingers and a million pounds appears as if by magic. Rugby league – a way of life to thousands of people – was never fair.

THIRTEEN

Nothing but the best

The modern-day rugby league player is faster, fitter, more skilful and more athletic than players in the past. That is what the propaganda machine would have us believe. And it's a bloody insult to some great players. Faster than people like Dick Huddart, the big Cumbrian forward who was as quick as any second-row forward in the game today? Or fitter than the fanatical Vince Karalius who ran fourteen miles to and from training sessions after putting in a full day's work at his scrap-metal business? And all the miners, hod-carriers and bricklayers who worked six days a week, trained on top of that and played in more than fifty brutal matches through the mud and ice of winter? And more athletic than Tom Van Vollenhoven, the spring-heeled Springbok?

Perhaps they are better at lifting weights, doing a hundred push-ups or climbing trees in 'bonding' camps, but then all the mod cons weren't available to the players of the 1960s and 1970s. We had to make use of the sand dunes at

Southport for our cross-country training. I always told my players that if the Southport sands were good enough for Red Rum to use as a training ground they were good enough for us.

As for being more skilful, well, I could take that personally but instead I will say that I cannot think of one player I played with or against who would find today's game-plan of five drives and a kick anything more than a doddle. Faster, fitter, more athletic and more skilful? I think not.

So I make no apologies for not including any of today's players in The Team Of The Best Thirteen I Ever Saw, Played With Or Against. My Dream Team. In fact, I could probably name half a dozen such teams before I would have to look to a modern player to fill one of the positions.

Naturally, the younger fans of today who have just joined the family of rugby league supporters will howl: 'Well, he would say that, wouldn't he?'

In my defence – if I should need any – I can only say that I have always had the knack of spotting a world-class player when watching the game. Some people in life have that ability and I learned at the shoulder of the master – Jim Sullivan – so I can honestly say that the following XIII had the fitness, speed, athleticism and skill to take the modern game by storm. And they would not need unlimited substitutes playing stints of ten minutes at a time before needing a rest to do it, either.

So, without further offending today's international players and their agents, I give you the following as my idea of the greatest the game has ever seen and leave the pub arguments to you to settle.

Full-back: CLIVE CHURCHILL

The Little Master. It hurts to leave out my old mentor Jim Sullivan and Wigan's Martin Ryan, but Churchill, the Australian from South Sydney, was the finest of them all. He was hardly a giant – only five foot seven and barely twelve stone – but his tackles were bonecrunchers and his ability to find touch with long raking kicks had the opposition turning and back-pedalling. He had a bit of devil in him and he led from the front. He captained Australia, playing in 13 Tests against Great Britain. I was only an impressionable schoolboy when Churchill was at his peak but I have never seen or met anybody since who could take over as the world's number-one full-back. His tremendous defence, his kicking ability, his eye for an opening and his liking for attack – something he shared with Martin Ryan – set him apart.

Right-wing: BILLY BOSTON

I know there will be at least twenty wingers, ancient and modern, whom many good judges would say are impossible to leave out of any team. But you can only have two, and even allowing for Brian Bevan's record 796 tries – a performance that will never be bettered as long as the game is played – I have to leave him out. The same goes for my good friend Mick Sullivan, joint holder of the most Great Britain Test caps with 46 appearances. Bevan and Sullivan, two of the greatest wingers who ever graced the game – but still not in Murphy's Team!

Billy B was simply a giant, not only in size and stature but in his all-round ability. Some wingers can just run – and there are about twenty human equivalents of a Derby winner I could have named who can do that – but Boston was much more than just a finisher. He had strength enough to put the frighteners on most opponents, his tackling quality was up there with the best of them, and if he couldn't go round the opposition he would go through them. Ask anybody who has had to tackle Boston for eighty minutes and they will tell you how much it hurt to face the Welshman.

Still a legend in Wigan, Boston signed for the club when he was eighteen and had played only a handful of matches when he was named in the Tour squad of 1954. He scored 571 tries to confirm that rugby union's loss was rugby league's gain.

Left-wing: TOM VAN VOLLENHOVEN

Another convert from the fifteen-a-side code, the South African cost St Helens £8,000 and was worth every penny (even though, as I said before, he didn't know how to play the ball properly when he arrived!). A perfectly balanced athlete who could run a hundred yards faster than most, the former Springbok rugby union international is still adored in St Helens. He scored the finest try I have ever seen. It came against Hunslet in a Championship match at Bradford when he took on the entire Hunslet team with a seventy-five-yard run down the wing, beating four players without straying more than a couple of yards in-field. He could break tackles almost at will – he had to be a quick learner following his first-day experience against Pat Quinn of Leeds – and, like Boston, was more than capable of doing his share of the tackling. He is probably best remembered for his Wembley try of 1961 when he went on a ninety-yard run, inter-passing with Ken Large, to help beat Wigan 12–6.

His ten-year career produced 397 tries – he achieved the remarkable feat of twice scoring six in a match – and a host of great memories.

Centre: REG GASNIER

Simply the best. Reg was the greatest centre I ever saw, and I played with and against some greats. There was something special about him . . . something that set him apart from other players. Sure, he had that extra and vital ingredient of speed and he had the right build for a centre but he had much more.

Gasnier was an entertainer. People would pay good money to see him perform – even when he was single-handedly destroying the Test dreams of Great Britain and the home fans. His ability to break out of almost any tackle earned him the nickname 'Puff the Magic Dragon' in the Australian press.

Even when he came face to face with two of Britain's finest, Eric Ashton and Alan Davies, Gasnier took the game by storm, scoring a hat-trick of tries, so that wherever he went he was the centre of attention. Ashton, whom I find extremely hard to leave out of my Dream Team, got his own back on young Gasnier during the 1962 tour Down Under, making him look less than the genius he really was, but a year later he was back carrying out the job he loved best – beating Great Britain. A hat-trick at Wembley, a major role in the record win at Swinton, and Gasnier ruled the roost again. His career ended when he broke his leg on his third Tour in 1967 but by then he had left an indelible mark on centre play. We have never seen anybody like him since.

Centre: HARRY WELLS

Wells, another Australian, would be the man I would choose to partner Gasnier, putting him alongside Boston to provide the balance. Wells was big and strong and rarely got the credit he deserved. He was not as fast as Gasnier but he was still a superb player in his own right and was not somebody you would like to come up against too often. He took a lot of the weight off Gasnier's shoulders and he did much to help make his partner the player he was. The inclusion of Wells means no place for Ashton, Alan Davies, Phil Jackson and Lewis Jones – and I haven't seen a modern player whom I feel guilty about leaving out.

Stand-off: DAVID BOLTON
This was the toughest decision I had to make: Bolton or Brett Kenny. A product of the recent past – he flourished in the 1980s – Kenny was my kind of stand-off, a real laid-back character who earned the nickname Joe Cool. He had his critics, especially for his slouching, gum-chewing appearance during the formal introductions to the 1985 final. He then went on to lift the Lance Todd Trophy. That was typical Brett Kenny, a player who had time and the class to use it. Not far behind was Wally Lewis – The Emperor himself. Great players, both of them, but I plumped for David Bolton, not because he was necessarily a greater player than either of the two Australians but he had speed in abundance. There were not many as quick off the mark as I was but Bolton came pretty close. If I made a break I could guarantee that the man backing me up would be the Wigan stand-off. He emigrated to Australia, and did a great job for Balmain. I would choose him as a partner in any era.

Which brings me to . . .

Scrum-half: ME
Well, who else would you expect me to choose? So, it might look like the statement of a big-headed bugger but that doesn't alter the fact that I would be the best man for the job.

Pace was important and I had that. I also had the ability to get on the nerves of the opposition – vital in a scrum-half – I could score and make tries, drop goals and read the game as well as anybody. So I make no apologies for including the name of Murphy in the line-up.

Just so you don't think it was a one-man race, the nearest challenger for the number 7 shirt was an Australian, Peter Sterling. Probably not as quick as me, he was still one of the best scrum-halves I have ever seen, and his partnership with Brett Kenny was to my mind the best half-back pairing Australia ever had.

In picking a pack, I had to choose six men who could fill the job description. Prop forwards who could prop, a hooker who could hook and so on. The game of the new millennium has no place for such specialists; scrums are such a shambles that hookers never see the ball anyway, and are only second-hand half-backs; there's nothing for a prop to prop and the loose-forward hardly has to bend his back. Even so, I still think the following six would have been a sensation today because they could play rugby league.

Open-side prop: ALAN PRESCOTT
He joined St Helens as a winger from Halifax so speed was never a problem – he could match any of today's forwards for pace. He did not have the greatest pair of hands in the game and you could probably find harder men than Prescott, but I defy anybody to come up with one who has shown more courage than the captain of the 1958 Tourists. He commanded the respect of every player who played alongside him and although he was a reluctant prop (having been encouraged to give it a shot by the most persuasive of coaches, one

Jim Sullivan), he turned out to be the ideal man for the job. A quietly spoken, kindly figure, Alan Prescott won the Lance Todd Trophy for his Wembley performance in Saints' 13–2 win over his old club Halifax in the 1956 final.

Hooker: TOMMY HARRIS

A hooker's main job was to get the ball from the scrum. If that sounds obvious then ask today's hooker what his job is, and ball-winning won't figure anywhere. Harris was a ball-winner and, while I would agree that a hooker did not have to have as much skill outside the scrum, Tommy would be a sensation today. Quick off the mark from the play-the-ball, he always thought he was too good to be a hooker and fancied himself as a half-back. He had to be put wise on that point – a hooker who could win you more than fifty per cent of the ball was a priceless asset. Another Lance Todd Trophy winner – he collected his award in 1960 when his Hull side lost heavily to Wakefield Trinity – Harris won 25 Test caps (the most by any hooker in the history of the game) after moving north from Newbridge rugby union club, and played nearly 450 games for Hull.

Blind-side prop: BRIAN McTIGUE

The greatest forward ever to play rugby league, McTigue was also a boxing champion, having had more than fifty professional bouts before making his Wigan début. A gentle giant, he had the face of an angel and the instincts of a rattlesnake. A true gentleman off the field, you could not believe he was the same man once he had changed into his rugby kit. He was a brilliant passer of the ball (an art he developed while playing basketball) and a man with an abundance of tricks – a rugby-playing magician. But, while he will always be loved and remembered for his skill, there was a hard and sometimes humorous side to the Big Mac of his days. In one game on Sydney Cricket Ground, a scrum was forming deep inside the Great Britain half but we were still waiting for Australian Billy Wilson to arrive. As he staggered towards the scrum he collapsed in a heap. McTigue just grinned: 'I must be losing my touch,' he said. 'They usually fall quicker than that.'

He confessed that he had given Wilson what he described as 'a little dig' somewhere near the Australian 25-yard line. It was no place for girl guides when Brian McTigue was around, but I'll remember him more for his skills than any skulduggery. Another Lance Todd Trophy winner, McTigue was Wembley's Man of the Match, collecting the award in Wigan's 1959 win over Hull.

Second row: DICK HUDDART

Not only was he a big man – sixteen and a half stone with not an ounce of fat on him – Huddart had pace to burn. He is another who would have been a sensation if he played today. And he had the image to go with the talent, regularly parading around in Hawaiian shirts and sunglasses. As godfather to his son Milton, I got very close to the big Cumbrian, and it was Vince Karalius and I who recommended that St Helens sign Huddart from Whitehaven. He had a superb bodyswerve that was a nightmare for full-backs, and when he was in full flow you could always guarantee fifty yards off him. Gifted with natural raw talent, Huddart was rarely tackled with the ball – no mean feat in Australia, and just when the full-back thought he had him covered, there he was – gone!

Second row: BRIAN EDGAR

I can almost hear it now . . . Brian *who*? A Cumbrian, like Huddart, Brian Edgar was officially a prop-forward but he was so adaptable that second row was a natural place for his talents. He only made the 1958 tour by default when somebody cried off, but what an important addition he turned out to be. We roomed together and although he was a quiet achiever he was not slow to take the mickey out of my accent. 'That burr up thurr is full of furr,' was his favourite line – and that coming from a Cockermouth Grammar School 'marra' whom nobody could understand!

Devastating sixty-yard runs on Sydney Cricket Ground were Edgar's trademark, and his opening running style made him an ideal second-row forward whatever the era. He eventually captained Great Britain on the 1966 Tour (the one I didn't go on because I wasn't captain).

Loose-forward: VINCENT KARALIUS

There can be only one choice for me. I know that there have been dozens of greats such as Johnny Whiteley, Rocky Turner and John Raper, some of them probably better footballers than Vince – Gentleman Johnny Whiteley surely was – but any player who can earn the respect, admiration and fear of the Australians the way Karalius did has to be a player you would have in your team. They named him the Wild Bull of the Pampas for a very good reason. They just couldn't tame him. Derek 'Rocky' Turner hated losing at anything. I remember one match up in North Queensland when the midweek side – those not involved in the Tests – were losing heavily to a country team of enthusiastic but hardly fearsome locals. Turner, who had sat through the first half on the bench, eventually walked out to remind those players that they were not just fulfilling a fixture because it was on the itinerary. They were representing our country. As always, when Rocky Turner spoke, people listened, and the second half produced the big win he had demanded.

Johnny Whiteley was a different character altogether, a gentleman both on and off the field, a product of the old school of loose-forwards, a fitness fanatic with excellent handling skills and the perfect delivery. He was probably the best footballer of the lot. From Australia there was Johnny Raper of the all-conquering St George Club. A player with a huge heart, he had a deceptive run and all the qualities you need in a loose-forward. A great cover tackler, he had a bit more pace than the others and, although he was not as big, he more than tackled his weight.

Yet, despite all this opposition, I go for Karalius. He was more than just a fearsome figure brought in to tame bullying Australians, he was a skilful, athletic player who could be creative or destructive depending on the circumstances. Any half-back in the world, whether from this generation, the last one or the next one, would have loved to play behind Karalius. He was the ultimate professional who, like Turner, hated losing.

A lot of great names are missing: Norm Provan, Kel O'Shea – two of those frightening Australians; record tourist Mal Meninga isn't there; Ray Price, Phil Jackson, Denis Goodwin and others you might include in your team of all-time greats. But I reckon this line-up would beat the lot: Churchill; Boston, Wells, Gasnier, Vollenhoven; Bolton, Murphy; Prescott, Harris, McTigue; Huddart, Edgar, Karalius.

Let the arguments begin . . .

FOURTEEN

Blow for blow:
the refs could take it

There's a story going round that during his playing days –
and later when he was a coach – Alex Murphy used to stick
pins in little dolls dressed as referees. Not true. If I had
anything to say about a referee, I would say it to his face . . .
which landed me in more trouble than sticking pins in dolls
could ever do.

I was often accused of trying to referee any match I played
in, but that is an accusation that has been levelled at most
scrum-halves down the years, and none of them will
apologise for that. But I suppose calling the best referee in
the world 'a big fat Yorkshire bastard' is asking for trouble.

Sergeant-Major Eric Clay – actually he had served in the
RAF not the Army but the description matched his appearance perfectly – was the first referee to send me off for
fighting. Now, fighting in a rugby league match in those days

hardly merited a mention, but if Eric Clay said you had to go, you had to go. I gave him as much lip as I thought I could get away with and occasionally I overstepped the mark – like the time when I threatened to throw him across the carpark and brought his parentage into question.

It happened after a game against Huddersfield when I thought one of their players should have been sent off for a bad tackle on Vollenhoven. I was so incensed that I took a kick at the culprit, Peter Ramsden. It was in the bar afterwards that I spotted the referee and let fly. He heard me, made a note, and I was banned for abusing him. At the time I couldn't imagine what part of the description had upset him.

Clay and I had many more run-ins over the years but, despite his bulk and apparent weight problem, he was always there to make the decision – like that famous day in the Cup against Hull KR when I scored the disputed try to win the match. I think over the years we just about matched each other in our verbal exchanges, though when I complained about him calling me a 'yapper', he still had the final word. 'Sue me,' he said.

Another in the Eric Clay mould was Billy Thompson, also a Yorkshireman. Billy, long retired now but still a hit on the after-dinner-speech circuit, tells a story about the thin walls between the dressing-rooms at Leigh. After one game during which, according to Billy, I had been screaming and bawling instructions from the bench, he was quietly minding his own business and changing into his civvies when, from the home dressing-room, he heard me shouting at the team for what I obviously thought was a pathetic effort.

'As for you,' I am supposed to have said to some poor unfortunate, so Billy's story goes, 'don't bother getting changed. Just pick up your boots and get out of my sight. Bugger the transfer list . . . I don't want to see you around this club again!'

If what Billy says is true then I owe an unknown long-retired Leigh player an apology. If it isn't, well, at least it fits into the image that has been built up of Murph the Mouth over the years. And it must be good for Billy's business.

Even after that 1971 Cup final when Billy had to face up to the jibes that he had been conned by Murphy, I always respected him and I think the feeling was mutual. Why else would he agree to referee my testimonial and then, halfway through, hand me the whistle while he played part of the game? I could have unleashed all the dogs on him that day, but such was the fellowship of rugby league that even your sworn enemy in black on a Saturday could become your best friend over a drink by Sunday.

Another of the top referees of the time was Fred Lindop. Unfortunately, Fred was never quite the popular figure the others became but he was a man you had to get to know. I did – and what I found out I liked. I always thought Fred was a bit of a poseur when he started – I even told him he ought to throw his whistle away and take up male modelling. I had my run-ins with him and gave him plenty of stick – he was the last man to send me off – but again I respected him and he was a good referee.

It may sound as though I spent half my life having a set-to with the man in the middle but that was the nature of the beast in me. I was a scrum-half who knew all the tricks of the trade and enjoyed every minute of it.

Just like players, referees could have bad games, but unlike today's whistlers they had to manage without the assistance of videos, slow-motion replays, in-goal touch judges, on-report facilities and all the rest. They were on their own. They earned the respect – and the abuse – of players but by and large they got things right.

Like the players, the refs I have mentioned (and there were plenty of others) were part of the game's character – as was one man who was neither a player, a referee, club chairman or director, a man who has had more slaggings over the years than anybody in the history of the game. Yet he is the one man who did more for rugby league in his day than any of the marketing men, chief executives or media managers will ever achieve.

When rugby league first hit the television screens, Eddie Waring was just the man the game needed. Perhaps he isn't in the same mould as the modern commentators such as Sky's Eddie Hemmings and Mike Stephenson, or even his successor, my old friend Ray French, but he did more to spread the gospel of rugby league than anyone else. Maybe his 'oop-and-under' and 'early bath' descriptions were a bit over the top, but he was rugby league from his pork-pie hat through to the soles of his shoes.

A columnist with the *Sunday Pictorial* and later the *Sunday Mirror*, Eddie Waring made household names not only of himself but of some players whose fame would not have spread beyond the boundaries of their own stadiums had it not been for him. Take Keith Hepworth as an example: good scrum-half though he was, he would not have been too well known outside Castleford had Eddie not cottoned on to the fact that he was a pigeon fancier; and although he might well have mentioned it every time Heppy was on screen, it gave him an identity.

The same goes for Roger Millward, another superb player, whom Eddie christened Roger the Dodger Millward. And

Don Fox, deep in the throes of despair after missing that crucial goalkick in the famous Watersplash final – so called because a torrential downpour had turned Wembley's famous green turf into a lake. It cost Wakefield the Cup. He will be forever remembered as 'that poor lad' thanks to Eddie Waring.

Eddie, though, was not universally loved. There were many who claimed he held the game back with his light-hearted quips, his outrageous accent and his references to pigeons. They believed he perpetuated the myth that the game was little more than a northern knockabout Saturday afternoon alternative for ITV's *All-in Wrestling*.

He once had a laugh during a snowbound Boxing Day match at Headingley when a dog ran on to the pitch and the producer gave it the caption 'K-Nine'. It was as though he had committed a crime against the game. He became Public Enemy Number One almost at a stroke.

Yet, Eddie, a former manager of Dewsbury, had travelled with the first post-war Tour party by sea to Australia in 1946, where he was regarded as the unofficial Tour manager. He was the one who got rugby league known nationally by pushing the game to the BBC and, if he became famous along the way because of that, good luck to him.

It was Eddie's love of the game, his involvement in that TV nonsense *It's a Knockout* and the well-loved but long-abandoned BBC Floodlit Trophy that gave us both the chance to have a chuckle. It was a cold and foggy night, Leigh were losing and all in all I should have been thoroughly miserable. Instead, I decided it was time to give Eddie something to cheer up the night. The BBC only televised the second half of their competition so as we came out for the second half I held a huge board in the direction of Eddie's gantry. It was the opportunity he needed, announcing to the viewers: 'I wonder what Alex Murphy will do to turn this game around – Arrghh, I see he's playing his joker!'

No, they don't make them like Eddie Waring any more. Ray French took over the microphone and his was the only voice of the sport until the arrival of Sky Sports and Eddie Hemmings and Mike Stephenson. They are not my cup of tea at all but they have a product to sell (it's funny how the arrival of satellite television turned a game into a product) so I suppose their gushing praise even when the game is dreary enough to make you want to switch channels is understandable.

Like referees and commentators, the press coverage has changed beyond recognition. These days, though there are more papers than ever, the writers have to struggle to get even a few words on the day-to-day news from rugby league. There was a time when people like Joe Humphries (*Daily Mirror*), Jack Bentley (*Express*), Alan Cave (*Daily Herald*) and Phil King (*Sunday People*) were full-time scribes devoted to writing about the game and its characters. The game may not have had its grand ideas for expansion in those days but it was healthy in its own little corner of the Empire. Times certainly have changed.

FIFTEEN

Aussies? I love 'em really

As somebody who over the years built up a reputation as an Aussie-hater – especially during my Murph the Mouth period in the *Daily Mirror* – I think it is time to put the record straight.

If I had to go anywhere abroad to learn about sport I would head Down Under. I have a great admiration for Australians because they are winners. What they don't know about winning isn't worth finding out, and the way they treat their celebrities and sports stars is enough to make the rest of us look on in envy. Not that we in rugby league get much chance to follow their example. And that's partly the fault of the Australians as well, because I believe that, in recent years, they have sold us short – and we have been soft enough to buy what they have been selling.

Nobody, least of all myself, objected when the likes of Wally Lewis, Brett Kenny, Peter Sterling and Mal Meninga came here in the 1980s on short-term contracts. They were a fillip to the game in this country and they earned every penny of their fees before going back to Sydney. When that particular fountain dried up, clubs over here looked else-where, and suddenly the Australians coming here were not the international stars we had grown to expect.

Ten years ago I warned that bringing in hordes of second-rate Australians would be a disaster for the game over here. Well, it's happened. Our standing at Test level is somewhere between the basement and the dungeon. It has never been so low during any time I have been involved in rugby league. This is not something that has happened overnight or over one wet weekend in Castleford. Anybody could have seen it coming. Ordinary players being paid extraordinary wages boarded the gravy train that was British rugby league. And with them came a bunch of coaches who, with the rare excep-tion, were as ordinary as the players. Yet we took them all in – and even went loking for more.

They came here to teach us the ways of the great Australian game, to teach us the skills and discipline and dedication that made Australians into winners. It was all supposed to rub off on our home-grown talent so that Britain would become a rugby league superpower once again.

So what have our youngsters learned from all this? Nothing. Ninety per cent of the imported players and coaches are earning high wages – not for the skills they can pass on, but for their accents!

If those who run our game were honest they would know that Australians don't let their jewels out of the safe. They keep them locked away while they offer us a few trinkets to keep us happy. Instead of the best china, we get cracked crockery. And if that sounds harsh and cruel, I make no apologies after seeing what has happened to the standards of our game as a direct result. Sad? Frustrated? Yes, I feel that, but most of all I am angry.

The imports are not capable of doing the job we are paying them for and the outcome is that, as an international force, we are a laughing stock. We cannot find two Test half-backs, or two props, or second-row forwards and, apart from Gary Connolly and Paul Newlove, we have no centres who would trouble the Australians or the New Zealanders.

The reason is that players who cannot hack it in the Australian League are welcomed here with open arms. They take up crucial positions at almost every club in Super League. It is about time the authorities put a block on players who are not current or recent internationals, otherwise they will go on stifling the game and our young prospects will lose heart and drift out of the clubs. Even now there are alarm bells ringing in areas that were league hotbeds in the recent past but which are now finding that amateur players are drifting away from the game. It is a worrying trend.

And, as I said, it is not just the imported players who are failing to match their publicity build-ups – the same goes for coaches. From my point of view nobody epitomises that more than Brian Smith, now back at Parramatta after spells at Hull and Bradford. Smith, with a CV that you would have to weigh rather than read, accused me of causing a mutiny because I had the cheek to voice an opinion about the game. He wanted me hauled up before the rugby league discip-linary committee for having the audacity to challenge his ideas. Perhaps I should not upset his sensitivities by challenging him to show me his medals. He certainly won none while he was at Hull. And he left Bradford with the job still unfinished. (They have done rather well since he went home, incidentally.) I don't recall the name of Parramatta

Eels appearing on the list of Grand Final winners in Australia since he took charge. Yet Smith came here as the great coaching guru; a strong-willed, articulate and highly intelligent man who could spin a good line. When it came to the crunch he was the type of Australian who is occupying too many of our key positions: a loser.

I realise that they can't all be winners but Smith's arrogant attitude that we Brits should be grateful for crumbs from the great man's table really struck a sour note.

In the 1990s the top clubs have been coached by a total of thirty-one Australians. You can count on one hand the number who have lifted any of the major trophies. A one-in-six success rate is a pretty expensive exercise in my view. Such unknown names as Dan Stains, Gary Greinke, Les Kiss, Peter Walsh, Steve Simms, Phil Sigsworth and Bill Gardner (Sheffield for a couple of months) have tried their luck without success. And even people we have heard of – Royce Simmons, Daryl van de Velde, Gary Jack and Tony Currie – have all finished stints empty-handed.

In the meantime, young English coaches are largely left with the scraps, trying to make silk purses for ever more demanding chairmen who haven't a clue what is needed and who immediately turn to the Sydney phone book for inspiration when things don't work out. So I make no apologies to Brian Smith or anybody else for speaking my mind.

Nor do I wish any ill on the likes of John Harvey at Salford who has been given an extended contract for keeping them in Super League . . . even though his pedigree from Australia hardly marks him out as a man destined to make history. Or even change my opinion.

The situation lower down the scale is hardly any more encouraging – clubs are Australia-mad. Rochdale Hornets got rid of first-time coach Deryck Fox – that is their privilege – and turned straight to Sydney to sign Steve Linnane. I am staggered that nobody has yet offered their head coach's job to Skippy the Bush Kangaroo! What is wrong with giving home-grown coaches a chance? After all, our international game is in ruins – Andy Goodway will be the man to pay the price for that because that's the way of things – but to hear the idea mooted that Britain may eventually look overseas for a coach for the national side fills me with despair. Have we no pride left?

I think that if I was an up-and-coming British coach I would be seriously tempted to chuck the whole thing in and tell the powers-that-be to get on with it, turn our game into some sort of academy for Australia. It's heading that way.

And despite the big sell that comes from Eddie Hemmings and Mike Stephenson on Sky TV, our club game is in a sorry state as well. The World Club Championships of 1997 were ample proof of that. Even our top teams couldn't hold their own against mediocre, middle-of-the-road Australian sides. Teams like Hunter Mariners – who went out of existence after reaching the final – were too good for Wigan. St Helens, littered with so-called stars, couldn't win a single game. Super League champions Bradford Bulls also lost every game. Likewise Warrington, Halifax and Castleford.

It is ironic that out of our meagre three wins, two came from clubs that no longer exist – Oldham Bears and Sheffield Eagles.

And what have we done since then to balance things up? We have imported more average Australian players to be coached by more average Australian coaches, and we have talked up our game, giving the spin doctors free rein to tell the world that we are closing the gap.

Well, the top Australians – that is those still playing and working in Sydney and Brisbane – know that the truth is a long way from the Gospel according to Super League Press Release Department. Talk about fooling all the people all of the time . . . somebody is trying to do just that.

Of course we never have any trouble filling Wembley – or Murrayfield as will be the case for the 2000 Silk Cut Challenge Cup – and the Grand Final at Old Trafford pulled in over fifty thousand in 1999. Local derbies such as St Helens against Wigan or Leeds against Bradford should be able to look after themselves without the need to give away free tickets. But what about the rest? A sport sprinkled with athletes who are supposed to be the best in the business should not be producing embarrassing crowd figures such as those that come regularly from London Broncos, Sheffield Eagles, Halifax and just about every club not pushing for honours.

If this sport is as good as we keep telling everybody it is, why are the grounds not packed every weekend? Let's get it straight: there is nothing wrong with rugby league – it is just that we have sacrificed quality to accommodate players who are, quite frankly, not good enough.

The door was opened to these imports with £87 million of Rupert Murdoch's money when Maurice Lindsay made the mistake of putting his faith – and the money – in the hands of the very same incompetent people who had landed the game in the financial mess it was facing when he struck the deal.

We have had our differences but I am convinced that Lindsay had no intention of seeing the money squandered on keeping every Tom, Dick, Harry or Bruce with an Australian accent in employment at British clubs. Most of that money has been wasted on player contracts and yet it seems that nobody is around to carry the can.

Boardrooms are filled with people who do not face up to their responsibilities. They will happily spend a couple of million pounds of money that isn't theirs and if they are asked to justify it they simply walk away and the whole game suffers. If they ran their businesses in the same way they would be putting up the shutters inside a year.

And if ever proof were needed of this, you only have to consider the example of Gateshead Thunder. Launched on a roll of drums and the biggest parade ever to hit the game, they are no longer – forced out of existence barely a year after the launch that was to take rugby league into a new age. The club has merged with Hull – reducing Super League to twelve clubs when since its very launch four years earlier all the talk has been of an extension to sixteen full-time, well-supported clubs throughout the length and breadth of Britain.

And the excuse for this staggering U-turn? According to Shane Richardson, their chief executive from Australia: 'We overestimated the amount of support the club would attract. The loss sustained' – reported to be £700,000 in the club's only year – 'was more dramatic than we envisaged. If I have let down the Thunder fans I apologise.'

The let-down for the Thunder fans, though, is hardly the point. The whole game has again been opened to ridicule by people with fancy ideas and expectations beyond the wildest dreams of anybody who knows anything about the sport. What makes these newcomers think they can make money out of rugby league by launching a club in Gateshead when after a hundred years' experience in the heartlands nobody has ever become rich on the back of running even the most successful club?

The outcome of the Gateshead–Hull merger – though as in the case of Huddersfield and Sheffield the word hardly covers the implications – is that £2.5 million has been spent on wiping out debts and propping up ailing clubs. And you must lay the blame at the door of people who simply haven't a clue what makes a British rugby league supporter tick. From nowhere these incomers have become TV personalities, preening themselves as though they are important, but it is now time for these men who have brought this great game to its present ruinous state to stand up and answer for what they have done.

It should be compulsory to have somebody in the boardroom who at least knows something about rugby league and not people who will fall for all the cheap claptrap and spin-doctoring that the marketing men use to get their message across. And if they don't know about the game they should mix with the people who do – the people on the terraces.

In the end, when the Sky money dries up, when all the hype and marketspeak merchants have moved on to pastures new, it will be left to the men and women who pay at the turnstiles to save this game. They are the ones who have been ignored or treated like second-class citizens while dozens of new jobs have been created in various offices from Red Hall (home of the rugby league) or King Street in Leeds where the offices of Super League (Europe) Limited occupy a prime and expensive site, right through to the clubs themselves with all their fancy ideas about selling the game.

I will risk the wrath of these people to scream loud and clear: 'The game's in a mess and it's all your fault!'

I am not opposed to summer rugby, but the question has to be asked after four years: where has it taken us? There are no more spectators coming through the turnstiles and evidence from the Tri-Series in Australia and New Zealand confirms that the standard has not gone up one rung – we are no closer to competing with the big two than we have been for years. In fact, we are further away, and all this in the year of the World Cup.

The problem is that the game, in its present form, cannot compete in the sporting arena in which it has decided to play – the summer. Cricket, year-round soccer, golf, angling, bowls plus a host of summer activities that have got nothing to do with sports such as barbecues, garden fêtes and holidays all compete for a spectator's time and money. And, even worse, some of the matches that have been served up over the last few years have been rubbish!

I have heard all the talk about standing on terraces, wearing a summer shirt and shorts with a pint in hand and the sun streaming down on a sea of colours. Well, that all sounds wonderful but it isn't rugby league.

The game has no stability – the contrived mergers and the failure to promote Hunslet to Super League because their ground and finances aren't up to the mark is sheer hypocrisy by the men running the game. Hunslet will never get crowds of ten thousand – so why do they need a ground that holds that sort of figure? And how many of the chairmen who refused them entry can go along to their own grounds and say they are treating their supporters properly?

Summer rugby, Super League, second-rate imports – they are all desperate measures to woo worldwide viewers for Sky Television. I am convinced that when Rupert Murdoch offered rugby league the mega-deal of £87 million he was looking for a TV slot, not a revolution that has reduced the game to a shadow of the sport that he bought – the sport that was the attraction in the first place. Super League make and break more rules over a twelve-month period than I ever knew how to do during my career.

This is a game that has probably seen more changes than any other sport in the years I have been involved. Biggest of all was, of course, the switch to playing in the summer and I am not the only one still trying to come to terms with that. Everywhere I go there are people asking me if summer rugby is here to stay. Who knows in the ever-changing world of rugby league?

And we have introduced such things as shirts that look as though they were designed during an explosion in a paint factory; a zoo full of nicknames such as Rhinos, Tigers, Lions, Cougars, Bulls and Wolves; and we have introduced squad numbers that make the purists cringe at the sight of somebody such as one of the world's best scrum-halves Shaun Edwards wearing number 47; and we have seen the arrival of pre-match disco entertainment, stilt-walking Al Capones and a variety of mascots ranging from the Devil Duck and Bullman to Ronnie and Rita Rhino. We have even had to witness a 'marriage' between two people dressed up as St Bernard dogs as part of some pre-match entertainment at St Helens.

On the field we have gone from unlimited tackles, to four tackles, to six; we've brought in so many different forms of scrummaging that hookers are redundant; we've changed the try from three points to four and the drop-goal from two to one; we have had such things as zero tackles and non-combative rucks; we have even introduced the hand-over when in the old days you would rather end up in hospital than willingly surrender the ball.

If you think that is all adding up to a long session of

bleating from somebody who played his international rugby in the so-called golden age of the 1950s and 1960s and is about to take a nostalgia trip, it isn't, so bear with me.

Not everything about the old days was good, just as not everything about the present is bad. I don't need anybody to tell me that today, as much as ever before, rugby league is the greatest game in the world. I have lost count of the number of times I have been asked to use a newspaper column or to give a useful quote slagging off the game. They picked on the wrong man. I love rugby league and want to be involved with it for the rest of my days. It may or may not be faster today than it was; it may or may not not be as skilful as it was – that is all a matter of opinion.

What is more than a matter of opinion is that those responsible for overseeing a great, exciting and vibrant sport completely missed the chance to turn it into the nation's favourite as recently as the late 1980s and early 1990s when we failed to make the most of the playing talent available, when we did not push hard enough to make people sit up and take notice of some great athletes. That was when we really needed the Big Sell and we didn't get it. We all claim to have the best game in the world – yet what has gone wrong? Why do we get excited by crowds of five thousand at some Super League grounds when Wigan and Saints were once watched by almost fifty thousand at Central Park? Now those fixtures are lucky to pull in fourteen thousand. If it is the greatest game in the world and better than it has ever been, why can't we get big crowds to the modern high-tech, plush super-stadiums that are all the rage? What have we done to fire up the public since we got our hands on Murdoch's money?

I think we have all let the game down over the past decade or so. We have had some great talent pass through our hands in that time and we failed to capitalise on it, to turn them into role models when we had the chance.

Football has taken a stranglehold on the youngsters of this country but there is still room for a second sport and that should have been rugby league. Instead, what has happened? We switch from winter to summer on a whim and we have not attracted one extra spectator. We are now floundering about trying to find our place in the sporting calendar while we compete with so many other outdoor sports such as golf, cricket, athletics, and every two years an Olympics or World Cup. The summer rugby brigade would have us believe that there is nothing to beat watching a match from the terraces, wearing shorts and a T-shirt. Well, for many people shorts and T-shirts are for the beach or the garden. I am not advocating a return to the dark days of bleak midwinter snows but let us dispel once and for all the myth that, until the switch to summer rugby, every player finished a game caked in mud so thick that he looked as though he had gone through a wrestling bout with a rhinoceros. Not true – if it was, how could Martin Offiah score more than four hundred tries in ten seasons of winter rugby, and most of them because of his blistering pace down the wing? And why can soccer clubs – who have spent money on improving their playing surfaces – go through a whole winter without having to slug it out through a ploughed field?

We have had some players who can stand alongside any of the game's greats. There are only nine of us in the Hall of Fame after more than a hundred years of the sport. It is just a matter of time before other names are added. A player has to have been retired for ten years before his name can be considered, which makes it about 2007 before the name of

Ellery Hanley will be added to a small band of players I feel privileged to be among.

But if we are not careful, the players of Hanley's era may be the last to come through. While we continue to stock our clubs with imports superfluous to requirements Down Under and at the expense of bright young British talent, I can see the game drying up at junior level. Our Test match record has been a disgrace for more than a decade – Australia have won seven World Cups and can probably only bank on New Zealand to give them any serious opposition next time around.

And all the time the generation of supporters from the 1960s, 1970s and 1980s are asked to believe that the product is better now than it ever was. That is definitely one for the marketing people to get their heads round. They have been given the privilege of being the guardians of a wonderful sport. Right now, they are failing miserably. It is time this game took a long hard look at where it is going as we enter the new millennium. I will, of course, be accused of scaremongering, of living in the past, of refusing to embrace all that is wonderful and beautiful. Well, I am used to all that kind of criticism. It comes with trying to promote a game that has been my life. But what I fear is that there will not be a rugby league game to follow unless we have a swift return to reality.

SIXTEEN

Get off the road to nowhere

It doesn't take much imagination to guess the reaction in the boardrooms to my accusations that the game has been sold down the river. 'Typical Murphy! Always having a go at somebody! Bucking against authority!' That sort of thing.

Well, I can live with that. What I cannot live with is the thought that these same people whose egos have been bruised by a few home truths could still lead rugby league down the same road as the dinosaur: to extinction.

When you have put your body on the line, for your club and for your country – and as I have already explained many rugby league games were serious battles of unarmed combat – I believe I am entitled to voice an opinion. And the Johnny-Come-Latelys know what they can do if they don't like it.

If I had my way the famous Room 101 would be filled with chief executives and players' agents. And I would throw away the key.

It was nearly ten years ago that I first warned that agents

would become a menace in the game. They bring nothing to the table, their only reason for being there is to take, to get the best deal they can for their client – the player. You might think there is nothing wrong with that and, in the words of so many of the agents, 'Players only have a short career and you have to make the most of it.'

The trouble is that the game cannot afford it – the agents know it, the players know it, and that expensive new breed in the office – the chief executive – knows it. But still the financial drain goes on. Together they are bleeding the game dry when their energies could be far better used to do their club and the game a great service. If every club had at least one board member with an inside knowledge of rugby league, we could take a giant step into a bright and – more importantly – secure future.

It is time the clubs stopped throwing big money at mediocre players, especially those from overseas, and went back to the grass-roots. I never thought I would live to see the day when Great Britain became the equivalent of a Third World rugby league nation, but it has happened. Until we go back to nurturing our young players and giving them the opportunity to develop, nothing will improve.

Every pound spent on an overseas player is a pound that could be better spent on bringing on home-grown talent. If you don't believe me, just look at the Test records over the last two decades. Britain's is abysmal.

I am not against paying good money to quality players from overseas but because rugby league is now a summer game such men are just not available. Anybody who is worth big money is already well and truly contracted to a Sydney club. And well paid.

For one hundred years rugby league has been a game

fighting for its very survival against a kind of bigotry that was nothing short of a sporting apartheid and against the establishment-backed rugby union.

And from what I can see, the men of the 1930s and 1940s – the butchers, bakers and coal merchants of the day – made a far better effort of it than the white-collar high-fliers who hold the game's future in their hands. And I have no doubt that the reason was a simple love of rugby league.

Today's agents and chief executives are, with few exceptions, like butterflies, fluttering from one flower to another – moving on when the first loses its appeal. Their love of rugby league isn't even skin deep. They have been brought into the game under the banner of that fading, almost forgotten document, 'Framing the Future', and I am not alone in thinking that they are doing a rotten job.

'Framing the Future' included the order to make big ground improvements for spectators in terms of seating, toilet facilities, food outlets and a host of other instructions. How many of these chief executives can say that they have spent even £100,000 of that £87 million on such improvements? Even Bradford Bulls, under the chairmanship of Chris Caisley, who is also the Super League chairman, can hardly claim that their Odsal Stadium is the first word in luxury. They boast regular crowds of fifteen thousand, yet how many of those customers can sit protected from the rain and in comfort? Less than a quarter. Bradford is a huge city and the club has known success almost non-stop since the switch to summer rugby. Those fans deserve better. Things are just as bad at glamour club Leeds.

Yet the money slips through the fingers of the protectors of the game and goes out to overseas and overrated players. Rupert Murdoch must sit and wonder what he has been given in return for his money. Heaven help us if he ever orders the game's governors to sign any document that forces them to be accountable before he agrees to send us any more cheques. I am sure he does not want all his money going on cheerleaders, dancing troops and Madonna mimics.

If this all sounds like a sledgehammer-cracking-a-nut approach then the message that the game is in dire straits has still not got through and the bullshitters are winning. The game, still a great spectacle, deserves better than that – lies and camouflage can't hide the truth for ever.

Players have to be encouraged to show more loyalty and be rewarded for results on the field instead of via contracts that the clubs cannot afford. And if they threaten to switch to rugby union as has happened in the past, it is time to call their bluff. On the evidence of the 1999 Tri-Series when Britain were thrashed by both New Zealand and Australia and struggled to beat two scratch teams, we wouldn't miss them. And rugby union wouldn't want them anyway because if they haven't made it in league they certainly won't make it in a completely new, unfamiliar code. Despite the seemingly bottomless money box offered up by mega-rich club owners, rugby union is in just as much of a financial mess as our game. And if discontented league players think there is a road to riches in the other code, they are in for a rude awakening. There will be no rugby union clubs queuing at their doors. It has taken that game less than three years to discover the harsh facts that the men in our own boardooms are still unaware of.

This is a plea from somebody who has lived and breathed rugby league all his life . . . a rallying call to give the game a boost in the new millennium. We must act now before it is too late or it won't be too long before we don't have a game to argue about.

Where, for instance, are the sponsors to match the loyal Silk Cut who have backed the Challenge Cup for nearly twenty years and will continue to do so until legislation rules them out of sponsorship?

Even Super League, that great flagship of the game, was struggling to find a title sponsor . . . further confirmation that the well is running dry.

And don't for one second think that a merged game will save the code from exinction. There are far too many in-built differences in the games' laws for that ever to happen. Rugby league fans like the play-the-ball, they abhor line-outs and rucks and mauls and the heavy emphasis on penalties. Union followers love discussing 'second-phase possession' and 'turnovers'.

If anything, TV moguls like Murdoch will probably put their money into a new concept – the third way which will be a hybrid rugby, leaving union and league to go their own way.

We must not let that happen. We must stand alone. Rugby league's hundred years of history, with that Rorke's Drift Test, Watersplash Cup final, Ashes series and World Cups – a history in which blood has been spilled and limbs broken – must not be allowed to go into the shredder. The great names of the past and the kids of the future deserve better than that.

SEVENTEEN

My way – right or wrong

Former referee Billy Thompson's memory of my yelling blue murder at some players after one below-par Leigh performance may or may not be true. If it came to the crunch I could always deny it, and after all these years there would not be many reliable witnesses.

But, on a serious note, there was one such occasion I cannot deny ever happened. It is in the archives of a Manchester TV studio for all the world to see and hear. It was during my spell at Wigan when Granada TV asked if they could do a fly-on-the-wall-style feature about a Wigan rugby league match – like I said, Wigan were starting to make it back on to the big stage by the time I left. Throughout my career I have been a warts-and-all type of person. What you see is what you get. I have never been one to hide behind a 'no comment' or, as is the case today, 'You had better see my agent.'

So when Granada made the request, I agreed; but I didn't

foresee one snag that would eventually come back to haunt me. I was the victim either of a set-up or of my own naïveté. It will probably come as no surprise at this stage if I told you that I am not the world's best judge of character. My wife, Alice, has told me often enough that I cannot spot a person for what they are. Friends have told me the same. And other friends – or certain people whom I thought were friends – have told me, if you get my meaning. So when I was asked to do the programme for Granada I thought it would be a straightforward feature that was part of every six o'clock regional news programme.

Not to put too fine a point on it, it was an effing disaster. At the end of the game the players trooped into the dressing-room. Beaten, their heads bowed, they slumped into their seats. It was then that I laced into them, accusing them of everything from high treason to animal cruelty. And if the Salford players thought I swore, they should have consulted Wigan. My language was choice and industrial to say the least. I didn't spare any of them – even those I thought were fine players. I questioned their spirit, their loyalty, their attitude, their ability – and every accusation was accompanied by a factory-floor outlet.

It was only when I had finished ripping away every shred of self-respect the players had that I realised the cameras were still rolling. Of course, it made great television – Murphy the Mouth in full cry, complete with all the necessary bleeps (dozens of them) to allow the programme to be shown in the early evening.

Worst of all was the fact that not only had I let myself be depicted as some raging dressing-room bully, but I had to apologise to my mother for the language I had used. I knew she would be horrified. Words that sound perfectly normal in the aftermath of a tough, physical game of rugby, when everybody is entitled to blow a fuse, is hardly the sort of thing you would like to hear in your living-room over your evening meal. And nobody would like his mother to hear it.

That occasion was one of my least favourite memories but any other regrets I have after half a lifetime in the game of rugby league are more for things I *didn't* do rather than anything I did.

Take the Great Britain coaching position for instance. Over the years my name has been linked with that job more than anybody else's. When things were going wrong, the message was 'send for Murphy'. The papers were full of it. Day after day I was touted as the man to lead Great Britain in an Ashes series.

I had an ally in the chairman of the International Selectors, the late Bill Oxley from Barrow. But when Peter Fox was axed after the 1978 series following a 2–1 series defeat by Australia (in hindsight that result was a mini-miracle) they sent for Eric Ashton to lead the Lions on the 1979 tour Down Under. The result: a 3–0 whitewash. By 1982 and the arrival of the Kangaroo team that was to be forever known as The Invincibles, the job had gone to Johnny Whiteley, one of the game's great loose-forwards. That year the Australians swept all before them . . . almost. The closest they came to defeat was when they scraped through 13–9 against Alex Murphy's Wigan in a game when, as *Rothman's Yearbook* reported at the time, 'Wigan sacrificed several kickable penalties in favour of an assault on the Aussie line.'

The Test series was, however, a lot different: a 3–0 whitewash. With Johnny Whiteley discarded after that series, my name was again on everybody's lips – everybody, that is, except the people who mattered: those who chose the coach. For the 1984 trip to Australia they selected Frank Myler. The Ashes series resulted in another 3–0 whitewash.

I suppose I must have known that my time would never come when, in 1985, the rugby league directors appointed Maurice Bamford, the man I had replaced at Wigan because they thought he couldn't do that job, to the position of Great Britain coach for the visit of New Zealand. The series against the Kiwis was drawn but Maurice remained as coach for the 1986 visit from the Kangaroos who became the second Australian side to leave these shores undefeated; and the Test series: a 3–0 whitewash.

If I had an inkling that my chance had gone when Maurice Bamford was appointed, it was a cast-iron certainty when they announced his replacement. It was Malcolm Reilly who was chosen to drag Britain screaming into the modern game. He halted the rot, just, by winning a Test in 1988 – it was the third and the series was already lost – but by then we were grateful for anything.

Malcolm Reilly and I have rarely seen eye to eye. I am certainly not his favourite person and he isn't a man I would choose to share a quiet drink with. I also believe that, unlike most of his predecessors, he had the choice of some of the best players in the world. It was during his stint as coach that Britain could select the likes of Ellery Hanley, Garry Schofield, Shaun Edwards, Martin Offiah, Andy Gregory, Kevin Ward, Andy Platt and Andy Goodway. Later he could add Jonathan Davies, Bobbie Goulding and Denis Betts. In other words, he had good players who were at their peak to pick.

Despite my reservations that Reilly is another who can only coach good players – something he has in common with Australia's wonder coaches – he is the man I would choose to get our international side out of the mess they are now in. He has been around the block a few times and has actually won a Grand Final in Australia. He was a great player and, despite his failure to make Huddersfield anything better than Garry Schofield, the man he succeeded, could achieve, he is the right man for Great Britain. Apparently, the players rate him and that has to be a plus. Britain needs a Reilly or an Ellery Hanley to get us back among the front-runners.

My regret is that I was never given the chance. I can only assume that I must have upset somebody very important along the way. The failure of people like Eric Ashton, John Whiteley, Frank Myler and Maurice Bamford before Reilly stopped the rot suggests that my name was well down the list of candidates despite the support I received in the press. I have never been told why I didn't get the job – but I do know for certain that it had nothing to do with my record at international level.

Throughout my coaching career in rugby league, I have often been compared to Brian Clough. 'Your trouble, Murphy, is you've got too much to say for yourself. You upset the wrong people and you'll never get the top job because those who make the decisions don't like to be told that they are a lot of boneheads . . .'

That has been said to me more than once. Brian Clough, who managed Nottingham Forest to two European Cup triumphs, never got the England job when everybody – the fans, the press – said he had no serious rival. I have regularly been referred to as rugby league's Cloughie and that is praise in itself. If he can live with the fact that less qualified people than himself hogged the limelight, so can I. Is it our fault that we know more about our game and how to pick players than anybody else?

The disappointment of missing out on the plum job of coaching Great Britain is something I have learned to live with. I must say, though, that I was angry about it at first – especially as my only coaching job at international level had resulted in just one defeat and second place in the world!

I was coach of England during the 1975 World Championship, a competition that, in typical rugby league fashion, was introduced to replace the World Cup which Great Britain had won in 1972. Britain's two league-playing countries – England and Wales – were split to offer a five-nation competition in 1975, and if ever there was a case for handing the title on a plate to Australia this was it. Instead of sending out our strongest squad, we split the team in half; and while the likes of Mike Nicholas, Clive Sullivan (who had skippered Britain to their World Cup win in 1972), Jim Mills, Tony Fisher and others were wearing the red of Wales, England were left with nineteen players who, with all the will in the world, were not the best Britain had to offer.

A combined team with me as coach would have kept the world crown on this side of the equator and who knows what that would have meant in the long run. But, even without the Nicholas–Mills–Fisher tough-guy triumvirate to choose from, we still managed to stop Australia when it mattered. In front of a crowd of thirty-three thousand in Sydney we held the Green and Golds to a 10–10 draw, and when they arrived in England we were more than ready for them, winning 16–13 at Wigan. The double over France (without conceding a try) and three points from New Zealand (a draw in Auckland and a win at Bradford) plus a victory over Wales at Warrington meant that England had beaten everyone.

So why were we not the world champions? It all boiled

down to the match in Brisbane when fewer than six thousand people showed the remotest interest.

If I could call one game back from history and play it all over again, the England v. Wales match of 10 June 1975 would be the one. Before the kick-off the match had been built up into a major conflict – the Welsh coach (Les Pearce) and the England coach (me) were involved in a slanging match that hit the headlines. Even if it was just an attempt to whip up enthusiasm it was given all the importance of all-out war.

Wales beat us 12–7 and that defeat cost us the world title. It is something we have never held since – or are ever likely to hold in the future. As England coach I had suffered only one defeat in ten matches but that was enough to get me the sack and deny me the chance to coach Great Britain in an Ashes series either at home or abroad – at least, that is how it will be until I am told any differently. So far nobody has had the guts to tell me why a succession of failed managers should get the plum job ahead of me. I am not holding my breath.

Another regret . . . While the fact that I was never asked to lead Great Britain will always rankle and I don't expect I will ever be told the truth about it, the one club job I coveted but never had the chance to take was at Leeds. Until they won the Challenge Cup in 1999 (against a totally inadequate London Broncos) the team they all said was from Millionaire's Row were the great under-achievers. Apart from a Challenge Cup win under Syd Hynes in 1978 they had won nothing worth having until 1999, despite the presence at various intervals of Great Britain coaches Maurice Bamford (twice), Malcolm Reilly and Peter Fox, plus David Ward, Duggie Laughton and Dean Bell as well as the less well-known Robin Dewhurst and Malcolm Clift. I am convinced that had they slipped the name Alex Murphy in there somewhere, Headingley would not have spent so many years on the outside looking in and envying the trophy-winners.

I cannot dwell on regrets from a game to which I have devoted my life. I may not like the way it is being run, I may think that the present-day player is overpaid and under-achieving, but I can see nevertheless that the sport has made some progress. Its image and profile are higher than they have ever been. These days the players can drive around in their sponsored cars, wearing their sponsored tracksuits and turning out in their sponsored jerseys. Good luck to them. Rugby is a short life that can be made even shorter with the wrong sort of injury.

It's a far cry from the days when I was at St Helens. I remember when sponsors first came into the game at Saints – a local company supplied us all with a string vest and the opportunity to buy a spare for seven shillings and sixpence as a special offer. Nowadays, string vests are out of fashion and it is all designer clothes and smart cars.

But while modern professionals have a lifestyle far beyond the dreams of the part-time player from the builders' yard, I doubt if they will ever have the memories to comfort them when they retire. From a personal point of view, three events came to end the century on the brightest possible note. First was the recognition in the 1999 Queen's Honours List. The award of the OBE for services to the game came at the end of a long (and at last recognised as distinguished) career and well after I thought such an honour had passed me by. It put cup medals, championship trophies and international caps into the shade – although without them I would probably never have received my invitation to the Palace.

There was another occasion – far less well known, less public and certainly not an event for the national news – that made me feel proud of what I have achieved and the friends I have made in the game. It happened at Wilderspool, soon to become the former home of Warrington. The club decided to have a reunion to celebrate the silver anniversary of their last Challenge Cup final win. Everybody turned up and most of them said they did so because they didn't want to let me down. During a career in a hard and physical game such as rugby league you make as many enemies as friends, but your friends stay with you for life. For somebody who is no longer considered important enough to have an opinion worth listening to – that's what comes of upsetting people – I can honestly say that enough people have a good opinion of me for me to believe I come out on the plus side.

If ever I needed confirmation of that it came in a recent phone-in opinion poll staged by the game's weekly *Rugby Leaguer*. There was no back-scratching involved, there were no favours called in, just the votes of the fans who had watched and studied the game for generations. Maybe the title was a bit pretentious – but isn't everybody doing Best of the Millennium competitions? The name that came out as the game's top player in the game's history – Alex Murphy. In boxing it was Muhammad Ali; in football, Pele; in cricket, Gary Sobers; in rugby league, Alex Murphy. It is an accolade of which I am very proud and one that reminds me of another award I received back in the 1970s. Perhaps England manager Kevin Keegan will remember it as he leads his team into the European Championships in Holland and Belgium. If he does, perhaps he will also remember that he owes me five hundred pounds from a bargain we struck at the Ladbroke Awards dinner. I won the rugby league award;

Kevin won the soccer prize – if either of us won the overall 'grand' prize we agreed beforehand to share the prize money. I hope Kevin doesn't have to wait as long for his first prize as a football manager as I have had to do for my cheque!

But, just as I bear Kevin Keegan no ill-will over the 'missing' five hundred pounds, I suppose it is time to extend the hand of friendship to the man who launched this life story. Maurice Lindsay is back at Wigan where it all started for him, and almost finished for me. Now a wealthy bookmaker, he is obviously looking for an easier life than the hassle and hustle of rugby league or Super League. Perhaps he has come to realise that he is not a one-man band, that the people he employs are there to do a job. I admire what he achieved at Wigan first time round – I am still bitter about the way he treated me but it is time to let bygones be bygones. As was the case when he and I arrived in 1982, the Wigan fans are trying to come to terms with a barren spell – they have just endured their first season for fifteen years without a trophy. On his return Lindsay promised a clear-out from top to bottom in his bid to bring back the glory days to the club. I am sure he'll do that and, if he needs any help from me, well, it's more the Saint than the Sinner in me to suggest he knows where I can be found.

Alex Murphy down the years

1955	Signs for St Helens on his sixteenth birthday.
1958	Becomes the youngest Lions tourist at the time of his selection. Gains the first of his twenty-seven caps in the first Test against Australia and scores the first of his sixteen Test tries in the second Test in Brisbane.
1959	Equals the British Test match try record with four in the match against France.
1961	Scores a try in St Helens' Wembley win over Wigan.
1962	Tours with Great Britain for the second time.
1966	Selected for a third tour but withdraws when he isn't chosen as captain.
1966	Becomes player-coach of Leigh for the first time.
1969	Leads Leigh to the BBC2 Floodlit Trophy.
1970	Takes Leigh to the Lancashire Cup victory.
1971	Wins the Lance Todd Trophy at Wembley in

Leigh's 24–7 victory over Leeds.

1971 Leaves Leigh to take over as Warrington player-coach.

1971 Makes his final Test appearance for Great Britain against New Zealand, ending a thirteen-year Test career.

1973 Warrington win the League Leaders Trophy.

1973–78 Coaches Lancashire to two county titles (1974 and 1975).

1974 Guides Warrington to the Challenge Cup, John Player Trophy, Captain Morgan Trophy and Club Merit Award.

1975 Leads Warrington back to Wembley where they are beaten 14–7 by Widnes.

1975 Coaches England to second place behind Australia in the World Championships.

1978 Warrington lift the John Player Trophy for the second time under Murphy.

1978 Leaves Warrington to take over at Salford.

1980 Leaves Salford to take charge at Leigh for the second time.

1981 Coaches Leigh to the Lancashire Cup.

1982 Leads Leigh to the First Division Championship.

1982 Leaves Leigh to join Wigan.

1983 Wigan win the John Player Trophy under Murphy.

1984 Wigan reach Wembley where they are beaten 19–6 by Widnes; Murphy leaves Wigan in August.

1985–88 Second spell as coach of Lancashire.

1985 Becomes coach of Leigh in February for the third time but in November leaves to take over St Helens.

1987   Guides Saints to Wembley Challenge Cup final where they lose 19–18 to Halifax.

1988   St Helens win the Regal Trophy.

1989   Saints go back to Wembley but are beaten 27–0 by Wigan.

1990   Returns to Leigh for the fourth time.

1991   Leaves Leigh in August and a month later takes over at Huddersfield.

1992   Guides Huddersfield to the Third Division championship.

1994   Leaves Huddersfield.

1996   Is appointed rugby football executive at Warrington with Australian John Dorahy as head coach.

1997   Caretaker coach of Warrington.

1999   Awarded the OBE in the New Year Honours List.

1999   Is voted the 'Player of the Millennium' in a phone poll by supporters and readers of the *Rugby Leaguer*.